Baldur's Gate II: Shadows of Amn

Baldur's Gate II: Shadows of Amn

Matt Bell

Boss Fight Books
Los Angeles, CA
bossfightbooks.com

ISBN 13: 978-1-940535-08-1
First Printing: 2015
Second Printing: 2017

Series Editor: Gabe Durham
Book Design by Ken Baumann
Page Design by Adam Robinson

for my brothers and sisters,
my brave fellow adventurers

CONTENTS

"Go for the eyes Boo, GO FOR THE EYES!! RrraaaAAGHGHH!!!"

—Minsc

A NOTE ABOUT GAME VERSIONS

Developed by BioWare and published by Black Isle Studios and Interplay Entertainment, *Baldur's Gate* was released for Windows PCs on November 30, 1998. Its sequel *Baldur's Gate II: Shadows of Amn* was released on September 24, 2000, with an expansion pack titled *Throne of Bhaal* following on June 21, 2001 to complete the Baldur's Gate saga. In late 2012, an Enhanced Edition of *Baldur's Gate* was released, developed by Overhaul Games and Beamdog and published by Atari, the current holders of the Dungeons & Dragons license. The Enhanced Edition of *Baldur's Gate II* followed in late 2013, complete with the *Throne of Bhaal* expansion. For the purposes of writing this book, I played these Enhanced Editions because they ran better on my modern iMac than the original PC versions I repurchased from Good Old Games, which then required some kind of PC emulation, and because the original Mac version I owned of *Baldur's Gate II* was no longer compatible with modern Intel-based Macs. The day before I finished playing, Good Old Games released Mac compatible versions of the original games, which I imported my saved games into for comparison's sake. But unless otherwise noted, all of the gameplay descriptions in this book should be understood to be from the Enhanced Editions of the game, which do differ in various ways from the originals, with widescreen support for modern resolutions and some minor changes to gameplay, including porting certain advancements from the later games into the earlier ones.

I

"Will you help me? We must join together once more, and our fury will be such that bards will run their quills dry! Yes, ink will be scarce where e'er we go."

—Minsc

IN A ROLE-PLAYING GAME, you start life already a hero. Or at least a hero in the making, guaranteed only to improve. Every scenario is designed and structured with your eventual success in mind, every storyline shaped to match your character arc. Everywhere you go there are obstacles but they are all intended to be overcome. None of your failures will be permanent, and unlimited second chances are always only a reload away.

The hero you play throughout the Baldur's Gate saga is known generically as Gorion's Ward, named for his or her—and therefore your—adopted father Gorion, the wizard who raised you in the library-fortress of Candlekeep on the Sword Coast of Faerûn, part of a world better known as the Forgotten Realms, the most famous campaign setting in Dungeons & Dragons. Unlike most of the other characters who will join your party, you begin *Baldur's Gate* as a 1st level character, a fragile and barely skilled neophyte in whatever class you've chosen. If you play as a fighter, then by the time you leave Candlekeep to embark upon the proper adventure, you might have nine or ten hit points, a mundane sword, and a suit of chainmail. Meanwhile, a mage could have only a single spell memorized, almost certainly Magic Missile, with its guaranteed hit and reliable damage.

When your father Gorion dies—murdered in front of you by an evil warrior named Sarevok as you flee Candlekeep—then true agency arrives. For at least a little longer, you are completely alone in this newfound adulthood, where even the slightest difficulty might be your undoing. Wandering the wilderness, you flee Gorion's murder only to find new enemies waiting everywhere: a wolf attacks from the trees; a blue-skinned, sword-wielding xvart charges across the screen; a gang of half-ogres repeatedly destroys whatever party of beginning adventurers you may have managed to gather.

For the first few levels of character progression, many player characters and potential party members can be killed with a single sword blow or spell. A 1st level wizard might have just a single hit point, which means every wound will prove fatal, leaving you no option but to reload and try again. Even after you grow stronger, the life of a video game protagonist remains a Beckettian existence: You die, you reload, you fail again, fail better.

In the first *Baldur's Gate*, Sarevok, your father's killer, is revealed as one of the Bhaalspawn, mortal offspring of the dead god Bhaal, whose titles include Lord of Murder and God of Death. After Gorion's death, you set out into the world to gather a party of adventurers, including the thief Imoen, your foster sister from Candlekeep; the druid Jaheira and her husband Khalid; and the barbarian ranger Minsc, a mentally-addled warrior who keeps a "miniature giant space hamster" named Boo as a pet, as well as the witch Dynaheir, whom Minsc was sworn to protect. With these allies and others, you eventually discover the many schemes Sarevok has put in place to upend the Sword Coast and to ascend to godhood in Bhaal's place. You also learn that you, Gorion's Ward, are another of the Bhaalspawn, with the same divine blood flowing through your veins as Sarevok. *Baldur's Gate* ends with the death of Sarevok—your half-brother— and *Baldur's Gate II* opens a short while later, with your capture and captivity in the dungeons of the mysterious mage Jon Irenicus.

BioWare, the developer of the Baldur's Gate games, was founded in 1995 by three medical doctors, Ray Muzyka, Greg Zeschuk, and Augustine Yip, but by the time *Baldur's Gate* was complete, Yip had left the company to return to his medical practice, leaving

Muzyka and Zeschuk to become the best-known founders of BioWare. *Baldur's Gate* sold extraordinarily well, becoming what GameSpy called "a triumph [that] single-handedly revived the CRPG." *Baldur's Gate II: Shadows of Amn* appeared just two years later, handily answering the high expectations of *BG1*'s fans with a game that was in every way grander in scope and ambition than its predecessor. With a score of 95 on Metacritic, *Baldur's Gate II* remains one of the best-reviewed games of all time, and won multiple Game of the Year awards upon its release. In its review, IGN said that "[t]he comparison between *Baldur's Gate* and *Baldur's Gate II* is astounding—like looking at a still oil painting, and then turning to see the scene in living motion on a big screen TV," adding that there was nothing to compare the game to, because "*Baldur's Gate II* has no peers." GameSpot similarly noted that the game had been "designed to be the ultimate AD&D role-playing experience—it features the most powerful monsters, the strongest artifacts, and the huge variety of characters, places, and situations that make Advanced Dungeons & Dragons so prevailing. […] It's a definitive role-playing experience, and the only reason it can't be called the best game in its class is because in a sense there's nothing available that compares to it."

If *Baldur's Gate II* was the "definitive role-playing experience" up to that point, so far ahead of everything else that reviewers couldn't even find a suitable point of comparison, then it was up to BioWare to continue to try to raise the bar for the genre. In 2001, BioWare released *Throne of Bhaal*, the well-received sequel-sized expansion which finished the Baldur's Gate saga by bringing the story of Gorion's Ward and the Bhaalspawn to a close. In the following two years, they returned one more time to the Forgotten Realms with *Neverwinter Nights* and its expansions. Afterward, the D&D license passed from Interplay to Atari, ending any chance for a *Baldur's Gate III* but freeing BioWare to work on other projects, eventually creating worlds all their own.

•

When I was a kid, I had little money of my own, nowhere I needed to be outside of school and sports, and no access to the broader distractions of the internet, which meant that left to my own devices I could easily play one game for months. Or listen to one album over and over. Or read the same books year after year.

My first Stephen King novel was *The Eyes of the Dragon,* a perfect crossover into horror from the fantasy my brother and I had been reading. And then came *It.* And *The Stand.* And *The Gunslinger.* I was hooked, binge-reading King and Dean Koontz and Clive Barker, intoxicated by their dangerous-seeming fare.

Reading horror novels, creating D&D campaigns, and playing video games about dark magic and murder was something my mother absolutely didn't want me to do—but she also never completely forbade it. When I first played through *Leisure Suit Larry in the Land of the Lounge Lizards*—sometime around the age of eleven—I didn't understand much of what was happening, but I knew I was getting away with something. As strict as my parents could be about certain things, they rarely denied us imaginative experiences. Even as a senior in high school, I had a very early curfew, but I could go anywhere I wanted in books or games.

As much as anything else, this was how I became a writer: reading, writing, playing, imagining, and inventing, often returning to the same stories again and again. In these stories I found I could have experiences other people did not have to know about, experiences they could not forbid or control. Books and role-playing games were a way to be somewhere else, to be *someone* else. As a teenager I discovered how you could be surrounded by your parents and your brothers and sisters, covertly thinking thoughts you were not supposed to have, safely having experiences so far beyond what anyone else expected for you they were not explicitly forbidden.

•

It is sometimes difficult to determine correct pronouns when discussing an RPG like *Baldur's Gate II*, where Gorion's Ward—the player character—can be of variable gender, race, and occupation. Who is the character and who am I? How separate are these entities? When writing about in-game experiences, are they happening to my version of Gorion's Ward or are they happening to me, the player? What should we call the character at the heart of our story? Sometimes I will say *I*, and mean either the character or me. Sometimes I will say *you*, and mean either my character, your character, myself, yourself, or some generalized ideal player. Sometimes I will speak of Gorion's Ward in the general sense, rather than in my specific case. There is no one right answer, and all these modes have their own nuances useful for the purposes of discussing the "role-playing" part of an RPG: Who are we when we begin such a game, and who do we become as the game proceeds?

What is it that forces us to venture out alone from our safe places, into the danger of the world? For me it was at first a barely-understood, barely-developed desire for *more*. By my senior year of high school, I knew I was sheltered, restricted, kept safe, a kid of chaotic good alignment not because I had chosen to be good but because I hadn't been given much room to be bad. But later I decided I didn't want to be good anymore, or at least not only good, and I also didn't want to live like the other teenagers I'd grown up among, who had by then mostly made it clear that I wasn't ever going to really be one of them.

Now, half a lifetime later, I understand that there are many different kinds of experience, and most of my own experiences can be organized into the broad categories of *lived life* and *art life*—and if I have spent more of my time in the second realm than in the first, this didn't make my experiences less valuable. The person I've become has been formed not just by direct experience but by the books I've read and the movies I've watched and the albums I've listened to and the games I've played. And then there are the books I've written, where I found that the time spent imagining my own stories was one way to live inside an experience of my own making.

Our lives are nothing more or less than the sum of the activities we've given our time and attention, and for the next hundred hours I am choosing to once more live my life inside *Baldur's Gate II*, moving through its rendering of the Forgotten Realms, into the simulation of that world powered by BioWare's Infinity Engine. I press a button. The world begins, and I am there too, a flicker of life inhabited by a tiny sprite in the center of the screen, waiting for me to move.

•

Most of my early gaming was done beside my brother Nick, the two of us sitting in front of our family's Commodore 64, then our IBM XT, our 386, our 486, and our first Pentium. Together, we progressed through generations of computer graphics, CGA and EGA and VGA and SVGA. We hustled for space on our ten megabyte hard drives, learning what DOS did only after first deleting it to make room for some game. We learned how extended and expanded memory worked through editing the system's config.sys and autoexec. bat files to try to twist games into the two kinds of space, a distinction I no longer exactly understand. We learned almost everything we knew about computers by breaking them to play games and having to put them back in working order to do homework. By middle school, we knew more about computers than anyone else in our schools, including our teachers. More than once we were sent to our neighbors' houses to help fix their computers, biking country blocks as door-to-door IT specialists, the way country boys of another generation might have been sent to do the neighbors' farm work.

For much of our youth, Nick and I did everything together, and most of our early video game experiences were had shoulder-to-shoulder, sitting beside each other at generation after generation of home computers. We watched the same movies: *Star Wars*, *Star Trek*, *The Last*

Starfighter, Indiana Jones, The NeverEnding Story, The Dark Crystal. We read the same books, in those years almost exclusively fantasy and science fiction, and later we played—or tried to play—Dungeons & Dragons together. In the woods behind our house, we spent most of our childhood acting out pastiches of the stories we'd taken in, using our shared imagination to fill the trees with orcs and enemy soldiers, to reimagine our tree fort as a dragon's head, complete with a slide we pretended was a snout we could clamber up or down. From the time Nick was born until I was sixteen or so, we were together more often than we were with any other person. Even my first memory—which is not a real memory but family legend—is of standing at the screen door of my grandparents' house, watching my parents drive away, headed to the hospital for my brother's birth.

Fabricated or not, my remembered life begins at the last moment I ever spent without a brother in the world.

These days, Nick is the unofficial curator of our childhood: He remembers everything I can't, and so immediately after starting this project I began texting him constantly, asking questions meant to fill the holes in my own record of our childhood together. Despite the many experiences we shared, our actual memories of those experiences have diverged. Our personalities made us focus on different things, and now, decades later, we both carry a partial story. Do I always assume his version is more accurate than mine? Maybe only because so much of what he retains is what I'm missing, perfectly filling the holes in my own memories.

·

The opening cutscene of *Baldur's Gate II* begins with a bound leather volume opening to reveal an illustrated version of the story so far, beginning with your childhood in Candlekeep under Gorion's tutelage, where you were raised with Imoen, "a kindred spirit, her own background as mysterious as your own." Returning players are reminded again of Gorion's killer Sarevok, your half-brother, whose shared parent was the god Bhaal, who foresaw his own death and walked the earth to leave a "score of mortal offspring, intended to be the fuel for his rebirth." You defeated your brother before suspicions about your own heritage forced you from the titular city of Baldur's Gate. At some point during your subsequent travels, the book says, you were ambushed and captured by a band of mysterious hooded figures, whose attack held "no malice or hatred, no mention of an old score, only quick capture and the promise of grim deeds to come."

The narration ends with a series of jump cuts touring the dungeon where you've been held ever since, showing off the cages your party will be found in, plus jars of preserved body parts, and trays holding scalpels and saws and other implements of torture. At last, we see a glimpse of our captor, Jon Irenicus, an as-yet-unnamed figure in a spiked skullcap, bent on torturing Gorion's Ward and his friends for his own sinister reasons. This grim dungeon is a surprisingly industrial setting for D&D—decidedly darker than the pastoral earth-tones of most settings in *Baldur's Gate*: The walls are grimed with rust, the floors are metal gates, bodies hang from the walls, and another cage holds a body long turned to bone. Surely, our fate could soon be the same.

Except there's no story without escape.

As the game opens, Jon Irenicus strides across the screen to stand before the cage imprisoning Gorion's Ward. He speaks, torturing you with magical spells between each line of portentous dialogue:

"Ahh, the child of Bhaal has awoken." *Magic Missile.*

"It is time for more experiments." *Lightning Bolt.*

"The pain will only be passing. You should survive the process." *Fireball.*

"Interesting. You have much untapped power. Do you even realize your potential?"

The torture session is interrupted when a golem enters the room and announces to Irenicus that "more intruders have entered the complex." Irenicus quickly teleports out of the room, just as a hooded assassin charges in to attack him. The intruder narrowly avoids two magical traps only to stumble into a triggered fire spell—a final energy ball from offscreen reduces the assassin to a skull bouncing across the grated floor. In the silence that follows, another door opens, and out steps Imoen: fellow captive, longtime party companion, and childhood friend.

"Wake up, you! Wake up! Come on, we have to get out of here!" Imoen cries, opening your cage. As she does so, the game's first journal entry appears, setting a few early goals. We need to escape, but the exits "might be barred by magic." Exploring the area could reveal how to remove those wards, but "who knows what traps this mage has laid or what guards he employs?"

I climb out of the cage. The user interface comes to life.

Nearby, another cage holds the half-elf fighter/druid Jaheira, a member of the fabled Harpers, an organization dedicated to preserving the balance between good and evil and between nature and civilization. Beside her, another cage imprisons Minsc, a warrior from the land of Rashemen, who in *BG1* acted as the bodyguard for the witch Dynaheir. Unfortunately, Dynaheir is no longer living, her body lying nearby in the spot where Minsc was forced to watch Irenicus kill her. Minsc is kind-hearted but mentally unstable, having suffered one too many blows to the head, and so needs to be tricked into breaking his own cage, after which he refuses to explain how he kept his hamster Boo hidden from our captors.

"Don't ask questions better left to aged sages," Minsc advises. "Boo is quick and evasive, and there is ever so much of Minsc to search; there is no hope of getting us apart."

To which Imoen replies, "Eww, I… really don't want to think about that too much."

All three opening dialogues between the starting party members introduce these characters' personalities and desires, but they also attempt to remind you of your previous shared adventures, creating a history which may not be the one you remember from the first game—if you played it at all. In a series built around role-playing and player choice, returning players may find it alarming to see their experiences in *Baldur's Gate* so cast aside by *Baldur's Gate II*. Even if you import your game from *BG1*, only your Gorion's Ward carries over into the sequel, stripped of his or her possessions but retaining the experience and levels earned in the first adventure. Jaheira and Minsc and Imoen were with me for dozens of hours in *Baldur's Gate*, but here they return in slightly altered form. Their character sheets are made unfamiliar by new weapon proficiencies and the strange contents of their spellbooks. They do not remember the choices we made together, will not be useful to me in exactly the same ways they once were. Whoever I need them to be, I will have to reshape them from new clay.

My first encounter with D&D was in a video game: SSI's 1989 release *Heroes of the Lance*, based on the Dragonlance novel *Dragons of Autumn Twilight* by Margaret Weis and Tracy Hickman. My brother and I probably played it at least a year after its release, off a copy of the game gifted to us by an older cousin, who handed over a pile of floppy disks and photocopied hint books at a family reunion. While we tried valiantly to master *Heroes of the Lance*, clunky controls and unfair systems doomed our efforts: It looked like an action game but behind its systems were unexplained dice roll mechanics and incomprehensible game systems, at least to a ten-year-old with no prior knowledge of D&D. As kids, my brother Nick and I rarely got past the first few screens of *Heroes of the Lance*, and even now, as an adult with three decades of video gaming under my belt, I don't make it much farther before I give up. In the late 80s, we didn't have access to online walkthroughs, so I can only wonder how much time my brother and I spent on the game, 25 years ago, trying and failing and trying again.

After *Heroes of the Lance*, Nick and I played SSI's famous Gold Box D&D games, including *Curse of the Azure Bonds*. The Gold Box games were brutally hard, and I'm not sure we ever finished any of them, although we played every one we could get our hands on, especially the other Forgotten Realms games and those set in the Buck Rogers universe. We came to the Gold Box games through my mustachioed serape-wearing sixth-grade teacher, who had a computer in the corner of the room loaded with computer games, of which *Curse of the Azure Bonds* was my favorite. I played often after my homework was finished—and I always finished as fast as I could, so I could play more. I was smart but I was not careful, obsessive and addicted in my rushing toward what I wanted to the exclusion of all else, and this was the year of sweatpants every day, the year of Velcro shoes, the year of the homemade Incredible Hulk t-shirt I bought at a garage sale and wore into rags.

That year, the same teacher made me a copy of *Curse of the Azure Bonds* to play at home, and he also handed me a disk full of the software necessary to connect to a number of local BBS systems, which along with my dad's 2400 baud modem gave me my first access to the precursors to the internet, a world of adults connected by computers. Almost all those adults were men, almost all older than me by at least ten years, and through the BBSes, these men introduced me to rural Michigan software piracy rings and to digital pornography so low-res and rudimentary it was about as arousing as a cave painting. Everyone was anonymous behind their handles and I never met any of the people I interacted with, but these relationships were the beginning of something that has stayed true into adulthood: Many of my closest friends have always been much older than me.

By my freshman year of high school, I had just one in-person friend from the BBS community, another boy who went to my school, who was in my boy scout troop, and who was on the wrestling team with me—where he wrestled heavyweight, his body nearly twice the size of mine. We would meet in his basement to exchange copied floppy disks and to talk about girls and games. I didn't really like him that much or necessarily want to be with him—I was just so grateful that someone shared my interests. Years later, I heard he was arrested for selling CD-ROMs of illegal pornography in the parking lot of an auto plant fifteen minutes from the town where we'd grown up. Later still, I saw him while dining with my wife at a buffet restaurant, flanked by his elderly parents, his body now even heavier. I don't know if he recognized me, but I didn't try to force the reunion. He was from a different era. I didn't want my wife to meet him, to see in him the kind of person I might have turned into.

Looking back, I don't remember feeling lonely in those years, although I must have been. Mostly what I feel is lonely in retrospect, a feeling that deserves a better name: What does it mean to look back on your life and realize it must have been worse than you thought? What is the opposite of nostalgia, where in hindsight objects and events can only diminish?

I also don't know if the other students cared what I was doing on the computer back in the sixth grade, while I was playing *Curse of the Azure Bonds* and other D&D games, if they were jealous I got to play while they worked. Would they have even wanted to be playing computer games alone like me, not talking to anyone day after day? Probably not. I mostly didn't know other computer gamers, although certainly other kids had consoles at home. By then I wanted most often to be left alone to my books and my games, to the thoughts that I believed were so different from the thoughts of others. While it would be a lie to say I never wanted to be accepted, most of the time I wasn't very interested in the world of middle school—which for me had mostly comprised of a sort of dull but constant bullying—or at least it didn't compare to the other worlds I had access to through novels and video games and imaginative play with my brother.

It would be another six years before *Baldur's Gate* arrived. But when it did, it would be instantly be elevated to the best of those video game worlds I had ever lived in, grander and more involved than any I had experienced before.

•

In the original *Baldur's Gate*, Imoen is the first potential party member the player meets. A foster sister of Gorion's Ward, she leaves Candlekeep soon after you do, joining the party shortly after your foster father's death. Cast as a cheerful and innocent thief in the first game, Imoen was a favorite character during my first playthrough of *BG1*, and has remained a member of every party I've ever assembled. Unfortunately, thieves are arguably the least powerful class in combat—their most useful abilities are picking locks and finding traps. Searching for a good rationale for keeping Imoen in the party, my brother Nick and I discovered that one reason to retain her was that we could dual-class her as a magic-user, allowing her to earn a few levels worth of thief abilities before progressing as a mage, a much more useful class. When we started *Baldur's Gate II* in 2000, we were thrilled to find out that what we had thought of as a story hack, altering the designers' intended path, had become canon: When you meet Imoen again in Jon Irenicus's dungeon during the opening sequence of *BG2*, she has become an 8th level mage, dual-classed from a 7th level thief.

As *Baldur's Gate II* opens, Imoen has been jailed somewhere apart from the rest of your companions, but she quickly reveals she's been tortured at least as harshly as you have, her innocence and cheer now gone. Your punishment was meant to unlock the power you carry in your blood, as one of the children of Bhaal, Lord of Murder. So why has Imoen suffered the same torture? Many hours from now we will discover Imoen is a Bhaalspawn too—and therefore not just your foster sister but also your half-sister, as *BG1*'s antagonist Sarevok was your half-brother.

Why didn't this come to light during the first game, when your own secret identity was revealed? According to dialogues later in *BG2*, Imoen's uncomplicated good nature kept the darkness within her from manifesting during the events of *BG1*—but Luke Kristjanson, one of the writers of *Baldur's Gate,* tells it differently in an IGN retrospective marking the game's tenth anniversary. Imoen was never meant to be this important of a character, and so her enormous popularity in the first game came as a surprise: "Her character was a late addition to fill a non-psychotic-thief gap in the early levels," Kristjanson said. "We had no recording budget left, so I assembled her lines by editing voiceover left from a scrapped demo... That's why she has no standalone confrontations/interactions with other party members, which makes her relationship to the player seem closer, and led to making her a half-sister in *BG2*. Make enough happen, and people see their own patterns."

•

As D&D games got more advanced, my brother and I got more advanced in the ways we played them. While the Gold Box games were still being released in 1991, the first *Eye of the Beholder* game also appeared from Westwood Studios, offering much better graphics as well as a change in perspective. While the Gold Box games had a rudimentary first-person exploration engine, *Beholder* used a top-down diametric projection engine for combat. *Beholder* unified all of its gameplay in a first-person perspective navigated with a point-and-click interface. The Beholder games were at least as difficult as the Gold Box games, and it was easy to get your characters stuck in situations where you couldn't advance. When that happened, the only options were to reload or restart, but reloading could only get you so far.

So we cheated instead.

Using a downloadable hex editor, I was able to edit the saved game files of my *Eye of the Beholder II* characters, adjusting their ability scores upward and giving them ridiculous amounts of hit points. Now years past the height of my computer programming knowledge, I find it somewhat incomprehensible there was a time when programs were simple enough that an untrained teenager could figure out how to do this on his own. I remember writing down all my character's stats, include select numbers that were easily changeable in the game, like the six ability scores, hit points, and total experience. Then I used the hex editor to search the save game files for those numbers, which often appeared several times. Back in the game, I would purposely allow a character to be damaged so their hit points would change, or kill an enemy so my experience would increase. Then I could open the hex editor again to search for the new value, using a process of elimination to determine which of the entries was the right one.

There is no way I would have finished *Eye of the Beholder II* without this trick. I am not entirely sure I finished it even with the assistance. But how can so many incomplete experiences be so memorable? To have read two-thirds of a novel or to have watched two-thirds of a movie would be intensely unsatisfying. What is it about playing part of a game that was enough in those days? And how long did it take to delve beneath the surface of these games, breaking them to get the kind of experiences I wanted? Where did I get this kind of persistence? How did I ever have that kind of time, and why did I spend it this way, instead of just playing something else?

Maybe because there is at least as much fun to be had in playing a game wrong as there is in playing it right. The best puzzles a game provided weren't always the ones the designers created for you, but the ones you created on top of the experience they'd intended.

Nick says he beat *Baldur's Gate* four or five times but only played *Baldur's Gate II* to completion once. I finished *Baldur's Gate II* at least twice—once on its own, and once again after *Throne of Bhaal* came out— with many other partial plays in the years since. And now I'm playing it again, beginning to end, for the third and possibly final time. But no matter how many times we play the game our experiences will not line up exactly. The game allows for too much variation, too much choice, too many options about where to go or what to do. There are experiences we will share along the way, but there is no one way to journey through the game. However you end up at your destination, you will eventually arrive at a victory that feels like yours alone.

II

"Yes, speak more of this evil-smashing partnership!"

—Minsc

ONE NIGHT IN 2010, the year I turned 30, I stood on a porch in Ann Arbor, having a drink at a party thrown by the literary magazine *Hobart,* talking with Matthew Simmons, a writer visiting from Seattle. When the conversation turned from books to Dungeons & Dragons, Matthew asked, "Didn't you use to play D&D? Have you ever thought of writing a D&D novel?"

Of course I had, I said. I would have loved to write one, especially when I was younger. But that night I probably tried to pretend those days were in the past, although I'm sure I didn't say why. In my mind, I was a "serious" writer. I wasn't going to write a Dungeons & Dragons novel—especially not before my first *real* book came out, my collection of stories already accepted and scheduled for later that fall.

"Too bad," Matthew said, "because I met one of the editors at Wizards of the Coast, and I think I might pitch a book to him. But it'd be a lot more fun to write with someone else."

Well, I said, immediately backtracking, what would it hurt to write a pitch? The worst this editor could do was say no. Probably he would say no, and then this would become just another funny story to tell in a bar, the time we pitched a D&D novel based on a boozy midnight conversation.

Soon after returning to Seattle, Matthew sent me an email laying out the skeleton of an idea. He suggested we write a retelling of Akira Kurosawa's film *Seven Samurai* set in the D&D universe—and together we started our outline, penning short backstories for a handful of then-unnamed characters, aligning their pasts with the new 4th Edition rules. When we were finished, we had an eleven-page single-spaced pitch, a working title, and a pen name—everything we needed to pitch *The Last Garrison* by Matthew Beard. A few months later, Wizards of the Coast told us they wanted to publish the book, and we were so excited we didn't bother to negotiate the contract.

•

While making our escape from the opening dungeon in *Baldur's Gate II*, my party discovers a room holding an imprisoned trio of dryads, who introduce themselves as our captor's concubines. From them, we first learn the full name of our enemy, the mage Jon Irenicus—a name, the dryads say, "that is synonymous with death and ugliness"—who has enslaved them so they might "instill emotion" in him, but the dryads say it is pointless, that Irenicus is "barren inside," searching "for something he cannot find."

Imoen tells the dryads that she thinks she dreamed of them during her imprisonment, and the dryads acknowledge this bond, saying that they know Irenicus touched Imoen as he has touched them, a likely reference to sexual abuse or rape, given the dryads' status as concubines. It's a curiously unweighted moment, one I was at first unsure if I'd misinterpreted. Why would the *Baldur's Gate II* writers include this suggestion if they weren't planning on exploring it further? But there are no dialogue options allowing you to express your concern or your outrage for your sister, no way to acknowledge this accusation. If Irenicus's possible rape of Imoen has any effect on what happens next, that effect occurs solely within the player, as the game never mentions it again.

We have no choice but to move on from further exploration of the dryads' situation or Imoen's trauma, and so we return to our escape attempt, eventually discovering the portal that leads to the next floor of the dungeon. We pause to take stock of our situation: Minsc's boss Dynaheir is dead, Imoen is traumatized by her own torture—and as soon as we proceed we find the body of Jaheira's missing husband Khalid laid out upon on a table, mutilated beyond the point where a Raise Dead spell might save him. At this sight, Jaheira vows revenge, and Imoen and Minsc and Gorion's Ward each vow the same, until all of our party is united by our shared grief and anger.

It's taken me maybe three hours of real time to explore this first map, carefully solving every puzzle and fighting every enemy, but according to the in-game clock, eight game days have passed, most of them spent resting to recover spells or heal injuries. During that time, my character has earned a single level, awarded mostly for experience gained in combat, killing mephits and evil dwarves and bands of goblins. This means that our journey stops while my characters level up, gaining more hit points, new combat bonuses and spells, greater resistance to enemy attacks.

I click on the portal and the screen fades to black before revealing the next floor of the dungeon, another maze of rooms between us and the surface above, another series of puzzles and battles meant to shape us into ever more efficient killers, a necessary progression if we are to succeed in our quest.

Even after accounting for the complexities of 2nd Edition AD&D, the Baldur's Gate games are still harder than most contemporary RPGs. Enemies don't scale to your level, and other than certain plot gates there's nothing to keep you from going somewhere you shouldn't too early, frequently stranding you in situations where you're unlikely to triumph. The game also employs a fog of war mechanic, limiting your knowledge of the playing field to what your characters might actually see, so there's almost no way to know an enemy is coming your way until it's already upon you. This often means you must reload difficult battles to better arrange your party before taking the last step that brings the next enemy into view, or kiting one enemy at a time out of a bigger group to reduce the challenge to a manageable (but story-breaking) experience.

Despite these tactics, the game frequently feels brutally unfair, and no matter how skilled you become at the game's combat, you will die often between waking up in Irenicus's dungeon and arriving at the final confrontation with our adversary. The dice will not always go your way, the odds will not always be in your favor.

Instead you die, you reload, you try again. After every battle, you loot the corpses of your enemies, taking their weapons and armor for yourself, stashing their magical items in your pack for later use.

In *Baldur's Gate II*, you are both the victim of great acts of violence and also violence's greatest perpetrator, killing your way across every realm you roam. How does the game's story account for the tension between the atrocities it claims its villains have perpetrated and the incredible numbers of violent acts the player is asked to commit? Mostly by pretending there is no conflict, no dissonance, no contradiction. Your enemies will be made to account for their evil, with you acting as judge and executioner, while your own acts will go unexplored, unpunished—or even lauded as heroic and rewarded. If there is a force in the continent of Faerûn powerful enough to try your character for the amount of death he or she has caused, you will not meet it in your journey through this game.

•

My first experience with pen-and-paper D&D came from my dad's copies of the Basic and Expert D&D box sets, which my brother and I found hidden high in our mom's craft room closet. By email, my dad recently told me he bought the gamebooks in college, that "they were likely there all your life waiting to be discovered"—but I've since learned this wasn't quite right. Contrary to what my brother and I had always believed, it now seems my dad bought his D&D books *after* we were born, when I was at least three and my brother at least one, as his editions of the two box sets weren't even published until 1983.

My best guess is that my dad bought the two box sets a year later, in 1984, after hearing about the game on television. When I asked him how he became interested in D&D, he said he became curious after seeing a story about "a student at Michigan State University [who] died while playing the game doing some real exploring in steam tunnels below the college." He said, "I was fascinated to learn more about what the game was doing that made it so he lost touch with what was real."

I had never heard this story, maybe because he wouldn't have told it so bluntly when we were kids, or because I hadn't talked to him about D&D in twenty years. But there's something thrilling about the idea that my dad considered playing D&D *because* it might offer such a powerful escape from reality. My dad, the straight arrow. My dad, whose sisters still tease him because he made my grandmother starch and iron his shirts for high school. Who I rarely even saw drink when I was a kid, and who preferred *Popular Science* and *The Wall Street Journal* to novels. It had never occurred to me that he might be interested in the same kinds of escapism I was.

By the time my dad bought the D&D books, he was already working at Dow Corning in Midland, where he'd stay until his retirement in 2010 and where I worked for eighteen months, before being fired in 1999. It's fascinating to me that the version of my dad who bought these D&D books had already been married a few years, already owned a home, had two kids, and wore a suit to work.

It's difficult to picture the dad I remember most from my early childhood—his suits, his briefcase, his eight-to-five workday, his weekends spent hunting and fishing—coming home to thumb through these D&D books. But it's also easy to forget that in 1984 my dad was only 29 or 30 years old.

Here in 2015, I'm 35, working a job that sometimes requires me to wear a tie and a blazer, and here I am buying the same rulebooks like my dad before me, using eBay to buy back childhood artifacts that I hope will restore more of my memories.

•

The popular version of the "steam tunnel incident" my dad remembered is a mostly apocryphal account of a doomed young man named James Dallas Egbert III, a child prodigy who started studying computer science at Michigan State University at the age of sixteen, before supposedly losing his grip on reality while playing D&D, leading to his death in the steam tunnels beneath the university.

The truth is tragic enough without additional embellishments: On August 15, 1979, Egbert left a suicide note in his Case Hall dorm room and entered the steam tunnels, where he unsuccessfully attempted to commit suicide by overdosing on Quaaludes. After waking up alive, he went into hiding at a friend's house, then fled to Louisiana, where he stayed for almost a month—during which he made another unsuccessful suicide attempt. A year and a day after his initial attempt, Egbert attempted suicide for the third time, this time dying of a self-inflicted gunshot wound on August 16, 1980—thirteen days before I was born.

It was a private detective named William Dear who theorized to the media that D&D was at the heart of Egbert's disappearance, and Dear expanded on this theory in his book *The Dungeon Master*. By then, a more sensationalist version of the story had already inspired Rona Jaffe's "problem novel" *Mazes & Monsters,* which depicted the "dangers" of playing D&D. *Mazes & Monsters* was later adapted into a made-for-TV movie starring Tom Hanks, and it was this movie that I believe generated my dad's interest in both the real life steam tunnel incident and the game that had supposedly inspired it.

My mom also remembered the story of the steam tunnel incident, but she remembered it having happened at Northern Michigan University, where I taught until this spring, and where my grandfather and my uncle were both custodians over the past four decades. One of the places we took our D&D books was to my grandmother's house in the nearby town of Rock, and Nick and I sometimes spent the long six-hour drive there in the backseat together, making up characters and storylines for possible play.

Reading the rulebooks on those long drives is a particularly vivid memory of our time with D&D, but how often did we actually play? Very rarely, at least in any kind of sustained way. There was just the two of us most of the time, and that doesn't make for a very good session. I spent insane amounts of time in prep, hoping to be prepared for the moment when I somehow tricked or ambushed my friends into playing: *If only I can set up the scenario right,* I thought, *this will all go according to plan.*

This is not much different than *Baldur's Gate II,* where often I had to save and reload to try to get my characters in just the right places, with the right kind of spells buffing them, trying to find the right strategy to win the most difficult fights.

Perhaps not so different at all, but while I eventually triumphed in *BG2,* my friends' disinterest in D&D was a puzzle I never managed to solve.

•

The deadline for turning in a draft of *The Last Garrison* was set just three months from the date Matthew and I signed our contract, but neither of us had ever successfully written a novel before. We ran into problems and missed the first deadline, then the second one.

I liked the *idea* of writing a D&D novel, but I quickly found I wasn't enjoying the actual work very much. It didn't feel like writing to me, not the way my other work did. Normally, I don't work from outlines, preferring to fly blind, at least during a first draft, and *The Last Garrison* also called for a different prose style than I was used to, a different way of handling character and plot.

More importantly, despite how much of my life I've spent with D&D, there was still a big part of me that felt dumb working on a D&D book. At 30, I was getting most of my fantasy fix through video games and movies, an arrangement that meant not confronting how much I still liked those genres, because it was only my taste in books that I judged so harshly. By the time we started *The Last Garrison,* it'd been a long time since I'd read a proper fantasy novel.

As much as I liked geeking out in bars with friends about our good old days playing D&D or our current video game obsessions, I found that the thrill of actually writing this novel wasn't sustainable for me. Months into the project, I still frequently felt like

I was just filling out an outline, and writing game mechanics into the prose felt like the worst kind of fan fiction. I wondered how to bridge the gap between what the book was becoming and what I'd hoped it would be.

In desperation, I went to my brother's apartment and borrowed stacks of the D&D novels I'd loved the most as a teenager—books he'd preserved after I'd stopped caring about them—to try to find what it was that had moved me when I was younger. Beside the old novels on his shelves were the rulebooks we'd bought together, pooling our allowances and begging for rides to the local hobby shop. By the time Nick and I started playing D&D, the 2nd Edition Advanced Dungeons & Dragons had already been around for a few years, so we later bought the *Player's Handbook*, the *Dungeon Master's Guide,* and the *Monster Manual*, the three books necessary to move us into that era. We bought the Forgotten Realms campaign setting, then the Dark Sun campaign setting, where we'd spend most of our playing time, and we read dozens of official D&D novels, one after the other.

We loved the Choose Your Own Adventure books, and those led to gamebooks like Steven Jackson's Fighting Fantasy series and especially to Joe Dever's Lone Wolf series. When our family bought its first scanner—I think this must have been somewhere between eight and tenth grade—I adapted the Lone Wolf books into my own D&D campaign setting, figuring out new character classes and how to rewrite Lone Wolf's Kai skills into D&D terms. I scanned all of the illustrations from the dozen or so Lone Wolf books I owned into the PC, then used them to create my own "Monster Manual" for the setting. This campaign setting is the only artifact I still have from my dungeon master days, the only copy secured in a three-ring binder in my home office.

In those middle school years, I also created a superhero RPG system from scratch, which I recall playing just once, with my friends. We played in my parent's pop-up camper, pitched in our front yard, and I can still remember how excited I was that my friends were finally willing to roleplay with me. I'd assumed it wasn't as memorable to them, but one of those friends still occasionally mentions it even now, with something like awe in his voice that I'd created this game from scratch. Here's another place where Nick preserved what I had not: When I mentioned it to Nick, he told me he'd kept the rules I'd written for the game. Around the time I was starting this book, he scanned them and sent them to me, and I learned that what in my memory was a hundred page tome was in reality just a few barely readable pages. How we ever played a game based on them, I'll never understand.

My brother still has the manual from our original copy of *Baldur's Gate II*, a 200+ page spiral bound book that includes, according to him, some of the clearest available explanations of basic AD&D mechanics, much better than those found in the official 2nd Edition *Player's Handbook*. This is another bit of evidence of just how good BioWare's Infinity Engine simulated that era's version of Dungeons & Dragons.

With only a few exceptions, I don't have any childhood photos, don't have any of my books or toys or movies, unless I bought them again as an adult. I left all of those possessions behind with my brother Nick, when I left our parents' house. Or actually earlier: when I left our childhood behind. We shared a room together until I was in middle school, when I moved into my own room. Before that, it was the computer room, and before that, it my mom's craft room, the one whose closet held my dad's D&D rulebooks. When I left my brother's room, I took none of our Star Wars posters or G.I. Joe figures with me. I was in the fifth grade, and I believed that growing up meant divorcing yourself from who you were before.

•

Early on, *Baldur's Gate II* attempts to strike a precarious balance between the violence that has been done to your party and the companions by Jon Irenicus and the violence you are asked to commit to proceed in the story, with your actions always being given less moral weight than those of the story's villains. The deaths of Dynaheir and Khalid—especially Khalid's, which is depicted more graphically—are part of what propels the party's revenge quest. But while Dynaheir and Khalid cannot be saved, the rest of the game will be played knowing death is not permanent for any of your party members, its effects always reversible by reloading saved games and through in-game devices like Raise Dead spells.

Similarly, Gorion's Ward and Imoen have been subjected to terrible violence, yet everywhere else similar levels of violence are both normalized and easily undone. Physical health is represented by each character's hit point pool, and the damage done by blades, blunt weapons, and spells all register as mere subtractions from this pool. It is very difficult to feel the damage you inflict and suffer, and the Infinity Engine's sprite-based combat doesn't allow for the kind of visual damage indicators more contemporary games often incorporate. Most of the physical damage you take is weightless, having no effect on you until you lose all your health: If you have 50 hit points, you are no less capable of a fighter than when you have 25 or ten or even one remaining.

When Irenicus tortured Gorion's Ward, what were the real effects of his attacks? The story claims your suffering was brutal, but when you step out of the cage you have all of your hit points. In gameplay terms, the first mephit you fight will do more damage to you than Irenicus did. This divorce between the gameplay effects of an event and the story implications is sometimes even more discomfiting: If Irenicus raped Imoen or otherwise sexually assaulted her, as the conversation with the dryads suggests, how can game mechanics possibly account for such an atrocity? Imoen has already been subjected to terrible tortures, and there are new horrors in store for her in the next chapters of the story. But her onscreen sprite idles normally, her hit points reading 57/57, and her status indicates no adverse status effects. Isn't she at full health, in gameplay terms? Whatever has happened to her, it will not prevent her from joining your party or from killing the countless enemies you will encounter together, just as she did in the first *Baldur's Gate*.

"Just like old times," Imoen says. "Except for the torture and all that."

Outside of some scattered dialogue and bits of narration, *Baldur's Gate II* tells you your characters are hurting only through the rise and fall of hit points through tiny icons that appear over your character portrait whenever you are poisoned or paralyzed or confused or fatigued or panicked. You cannot see these states in the sprites that represent your character—at best you can only imagine how these status effects might manifest. In battle, your character's portrait slowly turns red as you are cut, stabbed, bludgeoned, burnt, frozen, and psionically attacked, but every injury suffered can be reversed with potions, spells, or a quick nap in a camp.

There is probably a way to play *BG2* where you accept the permadeath of characters and move on. That is not the way I played, nor the way I'll play this time. I'm willing to push through the difficulty, fighting battles over and over until they come out right. I'm not willing to watch my investment in a character get lost because of an errant dice roll, but this is probably not the way D&D is really meant to be played. The possibility of dire consequences, more serious players might argue, is what makes a dice roll exciting.

Not only will you not be diminished, you will actually emerge stronger from your trials, acquiring experience points that translate into new levels and new abilities. Meanwhile, there is no character stat for trauma. For residual fear. A character who has been murdered by a drow elf and resurrected does not later recoil at the mere sound of the drow language. No matter how many times you die and are brought back, you will not suffer a nagging feeling that you are not supposed to be alive, that the sword blow or dragon bite

45

that ended you should have been allowed to stand. In gameplay terms, your characters can only improve. That which does not kill them literally makes them stronger, and almost anything they suffer can be reversed, then forgotten.

III

"We must inspire fear in evil! Quiet tales of hamsters are foolish, but a man and his hamster that tear evil limb from limb? That's scary!"

—Minsc

As we exit Irenicus's dungeon into Waukeen's Promenade—the merchant's district of the city of Athkatla, capital of the kingdom of Amn, a country frequently referenced in the first *Baldur's Gate* but never visited—the tunnel behind us collapses from the force of a magical explosion, a trope almost as old as video games themselves. On the rubbled remains, we find ourselves once again face to face with Irenicus, this time on more equal footing. Outside his dungeon, he's still engaged in combat with the mysterious assassins whose attack made our escape possible, but once we arrive they quickly fall to his magic. With their threat removed, Irenicus turns to us.

"So, god-child, you have escaped," he says. "You are more resourceful than I had thought."

"You're not going to torture us any longer," says Imoen.

"Torture?" Irenicus replies. "Silly girl, you just don't understand what I'm doing, do you?"

"I don't care what you're doing. Let us go!"

"I won't let you leave, not when I'm so close to unlocking your power."

Playing *BG2* for the first time, it likely appears Irenicus is talking to Gorion's Ward, or that Imoen is answering on her friend's behalf, as Gorion's Ward is aware only of his or her own ancestry as one of the Bhaalspawn. On a second playthrough, the ambiguity here is much more pronounced: This conversation between Imoen and Irenicus doesn't necessarily have anything to do with you, as Imoen is also a "god-child" whose power might be awoken.

Imoen and Irenicus conclude their conversation with a volley of attack spells, but before the battle can truly begin, it's interrupted by the appearance of several purple-clad members of the Cowled Wizards, a group of powerful mages who license and control the use of magic in Athkatla. The Cowled Wizards stop the battle: "This is an unsanctioned use of magical energy," their leader says. "All involved will be held! This disturbance is over!"

Irenicus attacks the Cowled Wizards but the battle is short-lived. Although Irenicus murders several of his would-be captors, more continue to teleport in, seeking to overwhelm him, and in the end he allows himself to be arrested, as long as the Cowled Wizards take Imoen too.

"What?" says Imoen. "No! I've done nothing wrong."

But it's too late. The Cowled Wizards cast a series of Dimension Door spells, opening teleportation portals into which they disappear with Irenicus and Imoen, who are now destined for the island fortress of Spellhold, an insane asylum for the "magically deviant" where Irenicus will continue to plot and where Imoen will once again face torture and imprisonment.

Up to this point, every player will have had more or less the same experience, with only minor variation. True agency begins here, several hours into the game, standing on a slope of rubble overlooking Waukeen's Promenade. In a novel or a movie, the next step would be suggested immediately, but *BG2* simply sets you loose in Athkatla, letting you choose your path forward. Down the slope awaits a conveniently placed noblewoman named Lady Beth, who offers some clues: Imoen and Irenicus have been arrested for practicing magic without a license, and while she doesn't know exactly how to get a license, you could probably inquire in the Government District. She suggests Irenicus's assassins may have been members of the Shadow Thieves, a local thieves guild, and mentions overhearing the "mutterings" of her stable boy, alluding to an ongoing guild war—"Thieves rule the nights," she says, "and war against those who would take it from them"— offering a clue to other factions you might explore.

Leaving Lady Beth, other options await. You are surrounded by shops, many offering new weapons, armor, and spells. A nearby barker yells, "Welcome to the Adventure Mart," hoping to steer you in his direction, while less than a screen away, a circus tent awaits, guarded by an Amnian soldier who explains the circus has been closed due to an incident during an earlier show. "Nobody has come out of the tent who went in for the show," the soldier explains, "and everyone we have sent in to investigate has not come out either. Foul magic is, no doubt, involved here." The guard will let you investigate if you think you're brave enough, issuing a challenge to which Minsc replies, "It is no risk! Not so long as we have swords and braveness to the brim of the tall glass of goodness!"

You might also take Jaheira's advice, who suggests you could head to the slums, where you might find "low-profile work" at a tavern called the Copper Coronet. Or you could explore any of the other districts of the city, visiting the Temple District or the Docks or the Graveyard, where many other quests await on the streets, down back alleys, inside of various mysterious buildings. Or you might do none of the above, leaving the city immediately to instead travel to the Windspear Hills to help free the dryads you met in Irenicus's dungeon by finding their Fairy Queen.

One more plot gate awaits before all of these choices will be ours. You can complete any quests you want to within Waukeen's Promenade, including investigating the circus tent incident, but once you leave the merchant district the game locks you into taking Jaheira's advice at least as far as the entrance to the slums, where you're met by a Shadow Thief named Gaelan Bayle, who takes you to his nearby home to speak in private. There he tells you his organization can help you find and rescue Imoen, but their help will cost you 20,000 gold, which you most certainly do not have. There is no real option yet to turn down this offer or to negotiate a better deal. You and your party members are marooned in a foreign city, friendless and alone, and this is the best offer available. You may hem and haw, but in the end you have no choice but to agree to raise this large sum of money.

Here's where the game offers its first bounty of choices, in the form of dozens of sidequests and optional adventures, some of which I've mentioned above. You have to do enough of these quests to raise the required sum, but you certainly don't have to do all or even most of what's available. Wherever you go next, your story diverges from mine as you acquire quests in the order of your choosing, finding new party members to recruit, new enemies to vanquish, new treasures to earn, borrow, or steal, with every new gold piece or salable gemstone leading you ever closer to being able to hire Gaelan Bayle to help launch your assault on Spellhold and rescue Imoen.

When we began work on *The Last Garrison*, my editor at Wizards of the Coast shipped me the 4th Edition *Player's Handbook* and the *Dungeon Master's Guide*, and the day they came I sat down to flip through them with more excitement than I'd expected.

As I understand it, most D&D players didn't take to the 4th Edition—and it's now been replaced by the 5th Edition—but I was impressed by the 4th Edition's relative simplicity, at least compared to what I remembered of the 2nd Edition. In the 4th Edition, pen-and-paper D&D had become very similar to an MMORPG, at least in certain aspects of its core systems. Despite remaining a gamer all my life, I haven't played many MMORPGs—just a month of the first Star Wars MMO *Galaxies*, then a little of both *World of Warcraft* and *The Old Republic*—but I thought I could recognize the influence these games exerted on D&D's 4th Edition, which I appreciated with a certain sense of irony. For decades, D&D had been providing the underpinnings for countless video games, and now video games were shaping D&D.

If I didn't remember exactly how to play D&D anymore, I figured I still knew how to play video games. The next day, I called my brother Nick, who at the time lived just a few miles away in Ypsilanti, a city bordering

Ann Arbor. He had been playing D&D again, now running the games as the dungeon master, and he had a steady group of players, including his wife Michelle, his brother-in-law Michael, and our younger brother Luke. I asked him if it was okay if I joined them, and soon we were playing once a month.

The first time we played, I showed up with a six pack of beer, assuming this was how adults played, and instead found a complete return to the tastes of our youth, a table heaped with Doritos and Gushers, Mountain Dew and Fruit by the Foot. But if the food had stayed the same, the game had changed: Nick used a program called MapTool to project dungeons he'd created onto his television, and we moved miniatures around a paper grid meant to match up with what he'd designed there. The miniatures weren't new technology, of course—miniature wargaming both preceded and helped spawn D&D—but they were new to me. I enjoyed the tactile nature of the game played in this way, but I also missed what I had always loved most about D&D, the communal imaginary space created across the table, a necessary creation when there was no physical representation available. The computer-generated maps and the miniature-covered grids made it easier to play with the new 4th Edition combat rules, but I'm not sure how much they helped the imaginative play I craved.

Still, in the same way the sprites in *Baldur's Gate II* can't possibly contain the complexities of their characters, neither could our miniatures, which always misfit our characters in crucial ways, leaving gaps for our imaginations to fill in what had not been provided. And for a short time, this was exactly what happened, sitting around the coffee table in Nick and Michelle's living room. I had never been anything but the dungeon master, and getting to be on the other side of the screen was immediately better than I'd hoped. Fifteen years earlier, I would have given anything to have had four friends to play D&D with. And now here they were, not friends I had to find but a party of adventurers already part of my family.

·

It's practically a requirement that you keep at least one mage and one cleric in your party at all times, and so the loss of Imoen can be particularly devastating to the party if your Gorion's Ward isn't a spellcaster. Thankfully, one of the first structures you come across in Waukeen's Promenade is the aforementioned circus tent, inside of which lies an illusory world created by a maniacal gnome wizard. Rescuing the circus workers leads to meeting Aerie, a winged elf who joins your party via some of the game's most stilted dialogue: "Aerie, should you be willing, we would appreciate a cleric/mage with your heart and nature." From there, it's off to the Copper Coronet, because in D&D there's always a tavern full of adventurers-in-waiting or quest-givers standing around, hat in hand. There we find our pick of several other new party members, each complete with his or her own quests: Korgan, a chaotic evil dwarven berserker who needs help recovering a valuable artifact from his former gang; Nalia, a mage/thief of noble birth with populist aspirations and whose family castle is under attack; and Anomen, a fighter/cleric who dreams of becoming a knight and whose sister has been murdered, a crime which he'll have to decide whether or not to avenge.

In the hours that follow, the game offers dozens of other sidequests you might undertake to earn the funds to rescue Imoen: In the Windspear Hills, a red dragon disguised as a human noble seeks revenge against you for Gorion's past transgressions. Back in Athkatla's Temple District, a drow priestess named Viconia (who you may have met in *BG1*) is about to be burned at the stake by a group of xenophobic fanatics. In the Docks, an outpost of Shadow Thieves is run by a traitorous guildmaster named Mae'Var, whose trust you can earn by working for an the evil wizard named Edwin, another returning character who sends you to assassinate his enemies. You might take down the mysterious Cult of the Unseeing Eye, or fight the ancient Shade Lord in an abandoned temple dedicated to the god Amaunator, or work for the secretive Harpers, one of the most famous factions in Forgotten Realms. There are kidnappers who bury people alive in the graveyard, wizards who will commission you to acquire the blood of dangerous creatures, slavers who Misnc will gladly attack, shouting, "Make way evil—I'm armed to the teeth, and packing a hamster!"

You can travel down nearly every street and avenue of Athkatla, and also descend below the city into catacombs and ancient ruins housing liches and other monstrous evils, or find the keys to astral planes and planar spheres, earning a trip to a demon outerworld located somewhere in another part of the cosmos. Succeed in certain quests, and—depending on your character class—you might take over as steward of a noble's stronghold or become the leader of a troupe of actors or find a druid's grove to serve and protect. As you journey between these quests, you will be ambushed in alleys, ambushed in forests, or ambushed in dungeons—often when you are deepest underground, desperately in need of healing and time to memorize new spells.

Because of all these sidequests, Chapter Two tends to be the longest part of the game, a disparity BioWare founders Ray Muzyka and Greg Zeschuk acknowledged in a design retrospective published at GameSpot. According to Muzyka and Zeschuk, one of the game's design guidelines was that the game should be divided into chapters, and that "each chapter should be of equal size and exploration potential," with a "rather obvious goal, but one that the player can achieve in any fashion that he or she wants." But the developers admit these guidelines weren't fully in place until the end of development: "[Chapter Two] included a story segment that was similar to those in other chapters, but in Chapter Two the player could also access all of the class-specific subquests. This led to Chapter Two potentially dwarfing all other chapters in length because the players could spend 60-100 hours doing subquests. We needed to put the subquests at a point where all players could access them equally, but the end result was that it bloated an early section of the game. In the end, there was nothing we could do to fix the chapter disparity, so we simply worked around it."

This "workaround" is, for me, the most memorable part of *Baldur's Gate II*, when the game is most alive with surprise and possibility, when there is the most to do, when your progress through the game is most directed by your own decisions. For the many hours you'll spend in Chapter Two, the game feels almost limitless, and its freedom felt truly revolutionary when I first played the game back in 2000, when the open-world non-linear gameplay of so many contemporary games was a much rarer phenomenon.

Eventually, my party gives up its freeform wandering to return to the Docks District where Gaelan Bayle's help will allow us to begin our search for Imoen in earnest. Outside, rain is falling. Two seagulls circle. A predictable volume of smoke escapes nearby chimneys. An Amnian soldier standing on the street corner says, "No trouble out of you," a fairly soft warning to my incredibly well-armed party. He repeats himself over and over, every few seconds. My characters turn their heads, idle their weapons while I write the above paragraphs. When I'm ready, we depart.

•

Despite the thrill of so much freedom, it's important to remember that the entire time I'm exploring Athkatla, Imoen is being tortured in Spellhold by Jon Irenicus. And it's not like I'm not reminded. At one point, we're shown a cutscene where Jon Irenicus breaks out of his cell in Spellhold and slaughters several of the Cowled Wizards holding him prisoner with a display of magic many levels above what anyone in my party could yet match. (Here's another of Muzyka and Zeschuk's design guidelines in action: "It is important that the player be kept informed about the progress of the villain.") As Chapter Two progresses, I'm shown several other dream sequences where Gorion's Ward watches helplessly while

Irenicus blasts Imoen with magic, all the while taunting Gorion's Ward to embrace the evil power latent in his bloodline as a descendant of Bhaal.

Here again is the difficulty of crafting a story in games that lets you wander off the main storyline. In a more traditional narrative, the characters would never spend all this time acquiring equipment and solving minor territorial disputes before launching their rescue attempt. What good is there in delaying Imoen's rescue, in letting a friend suffer unnecessarily? Presumably none. But because this is a game and because the game world necessarily revolves only around my character, Imoen will be no worse for wear when I arrive. There is no true narrative urgency except the player's interest. Wherever I go, the world bursts to life. When I leave, the world waits for me to return. Imoen is being tortured by a man I've sworn to kill but she will not be tortured any more or less based on how quickly I arrive.

In the dungeons of *Baldur's Gate II*, there are dead bodies everywhere you look, but someone has come along to reset the traps. The unspoken conceit is that this world was made only for the player. Everywhere you go, the world awaits your arrival. However the bounds of the game world are glossed, they are a way of enclosing the player inside a pocket universe, one in which every person, place, object, and event has been designed for the player's amusement. According to Muzyka and Zeschuk's design guidelines, "the story should always make the player the focus. The player is integral to the plot, and all events should revolve around him or her." This goal absolutely makes sense from a gameplay perspective—the designers at BioWare put the player's desire to wander and explore above all else, including narrative tension, which exists only when the player wants to rejoin the main quest—but a side effect of this total focus on the player's actions is the creation of a world that quite obviously does not move unless you are moving through it.

The Baldur's Gate saga excels at hiding this contrivance more than any of its D&D predecessors—but if you forget to finish off an early quest, you can go back to find the quest-giver waiting in the same spot. The incredible urgency of her original dialogue notwithstanding, she's done absolutely nothing to solve her problem since you've left. And why should she? It certainly wouldn't be much fun to play in a world in which no one needed your help.

Occasionally, I'm forced to leave the computer while playing to answer the phone or respond to an email, or else I switch programs, leaving the window running *Baldur's Gate II* to write a section of this book in Microsoft Word. Often I forget to pause the game, which means returning to find my characters looping their animations, weapons always in hand, always standing up, always ready to follow the next mouse-click forward, bellowing their want to continue over and over. When you leave the window, the world continues but sound mutes, so until I look back there's no way to guess what has happened in my absence.

But what has happened is always nothing.

•

In most Western RPGs of the *Baldur's Gate* era, the free choice between good and evil comes down to a choice between rewards: Often the evil choice causes more violence and results in more material gain. The virtuous choice sometimes allows you to talk your way out of conflict, but you tend to receive less gold and fewer special items. One favorite trick of BioWare's writers—I've also been replaying their *Knights of the Old Republic,* and it's everywhere in that game too—is for a character who you've just helped to explain that he'd love to offer you a reward, but he's just too poor. Often there's a choice to threaten the person you've just helped, extorting some kind of material gain out of him, which usually is forthcoming under threat of violence. So to be good is to constantly be giving up material gain.

While later iterations would become more complex, even in *Baldur's Gate* the worldview of the BioWare morality system is clearly visible, in its pleasing and often satisfying simplicity. Good players are rewarded in reputation points, which affect prices in shops, among other gameplay mechanics—while evil players get more gold and occasionally better items. This would be an argument for early-game evil—the more money you raise, the faster you can rescue Imoen—but there's so much gold around, and always more than you need once you're a dozen hours into the game. Most of the best equipment is found while questing, not lying around in stores. So is being evil worth it, in the end?

Here's what I know: In the world of Baldur's Gate, even evil characters can go to temples and donate gold to raise their reputations again. So maybe you can have the best of both worlds.

Because I so often use the quick save/load system to test out responses, I'm frequently able to manipulate the morality system in my favor. I usually play *Baldur's Gate II* as a good character, but if choosing an evil action will get me a certain slightly better weapon or a new set of armor, then I'll probably do it. I'm only rarely a villain in *BG2*, but when I am it's a calculated risk. And then it's off to the temple to buy back my good reputation.

•

Baldur's Gate II's Infinity Engine portrays the player character and each additional party member with a hand-painted portrait, which is used in the sidebar of the user interface, in dialogue windows, and in the character record screen. It also provides a pixelated sprite, which represents the character during gameplay and ingame cinematics, and in the inventory screen, where a slightly more detailed version can be dressed in equipment found in dungeons or shops. Character sprites are essentially undifferentiated: There are default sprites for each player race and class combination, and without weaponry or armor most characters look more or less like any other, except for minor customizations available for the color of skin, hair, and clothing.

Every character of the same race and class has the same haircut, the same blank facial expression too small to see outside of the inventory screen, and as the game progresses, other sprites repeat too. For every enemy type, there is a single sprite, meaning you're frequently ambushed by a set of identical gnolls, hobgoblins, or soldiers. Elsewhere, unique demons get their own names but then walk and talk and fight and die like any other, and by the time the game ends you will have been attacked by dozens of interchangeable elementals, trolls, beholders, mind flayers, and so on. Variations within a type of enemy are at best depicted by color-swapped sprites, with uniforms on a more dangerous breed of hobgoblin appearing green instead of red.

Back in 2000, I'm not sure how obvious it was to me that I found the roughness of sprites more inviting than fully realized 3D models, but in the years since I've often felt a creeping nostalgia for sprite-based games, as year after year we move slowly across the uncanny valley toward fully convincing photorealistic characters. Given the number of retro-styled games coming out from indie game developers, I know I'm not alone in desiring the deceptively simple graphics of earlier games. I can still remember the outsized investment of imagination that went into my characters in RPGs like *Pools of Radiance* or tactical games like *X-COM: UFO Defense* and *Jagged Alliance 2*, all of which had relatively simplistic sprite-based characters and enemies. Each of the sprites in these games took up precious memory, and had to be drawn by hand, pixel by pixel, one variation for every frame of movement, so what makes your enemies unique is not graphical differentiation but context and imagination.

Despite the lengthy story and the deliberate character-building present in *BG2*, most of your time in-game is spent not in dialogue or active role-playing but in watching your party's sprites walking from one edge of the screen to the next, doing your will with only minor exclamations, and frequently engaging in miniature battles with other similarly-sized sprites. For the game to be emotionally engaging—instead of simply a puzzle to be solved—the player must imbue these sprites with additional purpose and interest, going beyond what is given, as many players of the first *Baldur's Gate* clearly did with Imoen. But how exactly does this work? How do these barely-defined characters spur our imaginations to earn our affection?

Much to the benefit of the simulation in *Baldur's Gate II*, I rarely think of the characters on the screen as "sprites." Deep in a play session, I interpret the hobgoblin sprites as *actual* hobgoblins, filling in from imagination and experiences with D&D novels and game materials the requisite details, the yellowish eyes, the goblinoid features, the growled mish-mash of human and goblin languages, the brutality and aggression.

Part of what created this investment was a precise lack of detail writers call "flatness," a way of making room for the reader to fill in motivations, psychology, physical details, or other attributes of characters and settings: As you make the characters yours, equipping weapons and divvying up treasure and choosing color schemes for armor, or even just trying to imagine *why* your character might be doing the things the game asks him or her to do, you're also subconsciously thinking about the kind of person those choices might represent. And when certain traits seem to exhibit themselves during gameplay—for instance, in my playthrough, Minsc dies more than any other character, because he's my frontline fighter—you begin to fashion explanations for this behavior, imagining its effects on the character you've conjured in collaboration with the game.

In her essay "Fairy Tale is Form, Form is Fairy Tale," the writer Kate Bernheimer describes flat characters as "silhouettes," saying they "are not given many emotions—perhaps one, such as happy or sad—and that they are not in psychological conflict." Bernheimer praises flatness because "it allows depth and response in the reader," an effect which occurs in part because the writer has minimized the amount of psychological insight offered for the actions of characters, leaving room for the reader to create what wasn't given. In the most successful examples, this creates a striking effect, because readers will provide whatever the story does not, filling in the blank side of the silhouette with the best material they have to offer: their own imaginations, emotions, and worldviews.

The Baldur's Gate games, with their NPC party members that come complete with their own preexisting personalities and their own quests to complete, break away from the older D&D games like the 1988 Gold Box title, *Pool of Radiance*, which required you to create your entire party of adventurers. But even with their recorded dialogue and personal storylines, the characters in *BG2* still seem flatter than the characters in later, more cinematic BioWare games, where character models become more realistic with each game and where stories are fleshed out over dozens of hours of fully-voiced and lip-synched dialogue. (One casualty of this fleshing out? There are far fewer "mistakes" like Imoen to be had.)

The most memorable *BG2* characters each have fascinating backstories that lead to quests you'll need to undertake to keep them in your party, but much of this content is restricted to a very narrow part of the overall game experience. Across hundreds of hours of gameplay, you might spend little more than an hour or two taking care of each of their individual wants. For the rest of your time together, they will want what you want, go where you point, and do what you command. When they speak, it will appear as if they are interjecting of their own volition, but their interjections are triggered by your actions: If Aerie is not there to cheer your good deeds, then one of the other good-aligned party members interjects instead, Keldorn or Valygar or Mazzy or Nalia or whoever happens to be with you at the moment. Same goes for an evil decision, a betrayal or extortion or some unnecessary bit of violence causing Korgan or Edwin or Viconia to express their approval, often in exactly the same places.

Interestingly, most of the characters do have a kind of morality threshold, where they will refuse to join your party (or will leave it) if you become too good or too evil. This creates an appearance of complexity, but it's merely numerical. Their morality threshold is usually a hardcoded number, and as long as you stay one point of goodness or evil above or below, their final moral objection will not occur. These characters are only moral agents when the story calls upon them to be, and any additional depth they appear to possess is something the player has added. For example, if you've ever refused to betray someone in *BG2* because it wouldn't be true to your character or because you think Jaheira or Minsc would disapprove, then you've experienced the personal investment in character this system can create—your behavior is shaped even without a specific gameplay reward to drive your decision.

Another of Muzyka and Zeschuk's design guidelines that shaped the development of *Baldur's Gate II* was the idea that "it is important that the player is able to personalize his or her character. This means that they should feel that the characters they are playing as are their own." And so as the game begins, your player character is little more than one of Bernheimer's silhouettes, a blank ready to be filled in with your choices during character creation, where you choose your own race, gender, and class, plus your starting abilities, like weapon proficiencies and beginning spells.

At first, even your inventory screen contains only what amounts to a paper doll, a flat representation of your character waiting to be dressed up with +1 long swords and magic wands and suits of enchanted mail. Dressing up this paper doll is a big part of forming an attachment to the character: As you gain new equipment, you will of course give your character the equipment best suiting his or her abilities, but more than likely you also make aesthetic choices fitting the kind of character you've imagined as you played.

Gorion's Ward is the only character you create almost entirely yourself, and so paradoxically it's the protagonist of the game who ends up being the flattest character. We learn about him or her only through our actions and dialogue choices, and Gorion's Ward's speech is never voiced except for a few exclamations. However you end up feeling about the story's protagonist, most likely he or she is a character you've imagined yourself, spun out of the often-limited tools the game provides.

This effect is where the game most closely simulates playing pen-and-paper D&D, translating a series of statistics and an inventory into what feels like a living breathing person, a person whose life you have inhabited since the moment of their creation, an event occurring simultaneously in your mind and upon the character sheet or the computer screen.

A D&D character begins not with birth but with the first choice we make for them once they're let loose into the game world, or the first request we make of the dungeon master, or the first click of the mouse toward some destination on the other side of the screen. *Go here,* we say. *Do this. Fight this monster. Cast this spell. Open this chest.* Repeat. Hours pass. Days and weeks and months pass, command after command filling the empty vessel of the player character. Experience is acquired, levels are earned, new spells are scribbled into spellbooks, mundane swords and axes are replaced with deadlier magical weapons, and basic sets of chainmail are exchanged for ornate suits of enchanted plate mail. And then one day playing dress-up becomes something else. What is it you see when you turn the paper doll around in your imagination? Not an empty silhouette but a character coming alive, a container filled with you.

•

My car was in the shop the second time I played D&D with Nick and the rest of our group, so my wife Jessica had to drop me off at my brother's apartment. There was little dignity in being dropped off to play D&D by my wife, but the real crisis came when she arrived too early to pick me up. She came into the apartment while we were finishing the day's quest, a quest specifically designed by my brother to revolve around my character, a deva avenger, the same race and class as the villain Matthew Beard was writing into *The Last Garrison*.

My wife sat in the corner of the apartment's cramped living room as my brother and I roleplayed through a tense encounter with my character's ancestral enemy— an enemy who, in the best tradition of amateur twist endings, I hadn't know to even exist until that moment— each of us speaking in character, standing excitedly as we spoke, then diving back to the coffee table to roll dice, as the other three members of my party—my real-life family—tried to support my character in battle. I looked up occasionally to see my wife watching aghast from across the room.

On the way home, I burned with embarrassment whenever she looked over at me, an increasingly bemused expression on her face. She'd seen too much and we both knew it. Finally, she joked, "You know this is going to make you unfuckable for a few weeks, right?"

And so in many ways playing D&D as an adult wasn't different than playing it as a teenager.

IV

*"Give a man a fish and he eats for a day,
but teach a man to fight and he can chow down
on the meaty marrow of evil!"*

—Minsc

IN AN INTERVIEW IN *THE WRITER'S CHRONICLE*, the writer Patricia Henley once explained how fellow novelist Charlie Smith suggested that one way to draft a story is to first "write the islands," by which he meant the writer should draft the parts he or she already knows, those pivotal scenes that can be seen even before the intervening connective tissue has been imagined.

In many ways, *Baldur's Gate II* works in a similar way, by providing the islands and letting the player determine how they might be reached. For instance, every player will infiltrate Spellhold to free Imoen, where Irenicus will steal the souls of both Imoen and Gorion's Ward.

Next, you must face Irenicus's vampire "sister" Bodhi in the labyrinth beneath Spellhold, where the strain of constant violence and the loss of the player's soul unlocks a malevolent avatar of Bhaal called the Slayer, a manifestation of the evil you carry within you. During your escape, a shipwreck will strand your party in the underwater City of Caverns, a city ruled by the sahuagin, an evil race of fish-like humanoids, whose political infighting must be resolved before a route from their city to the Underdark can be opened. In the Underdark—a sprawling underground world, one of the most famous locations in the Forgotten Realms—you follow the trail left by Irenicus and Bodhi to the drow city of Ust Natha, one of the most difficult locations in the game. To gain entry, you will make a deal with a nearby silver dragon, who will disguise your party with illusions that make you appear as evil drow elves, and once inside Ust Natha you'll have to prove your worth to one of the city's ruling houses, a necessary subterfuge if you are to recover the silver dragon's stolen eggs so that the dragon will open the only path out of the Underdark.

Returning to the surface world, you find the drow now allied with Irenicus and besieging the elven city of Suldanessellar, which is not only under attack but also hidden completely in the elven forest, every path to its gates suddenly lost. Irenicus has created powerful magical illusions to seal it away, and only a magical lantern known as the Rhynn Lanthorn can reveal how to enter the city. Unsurprisingly, Irenicus and Bodhi have already secured this artifact, so the party once again has to pursue Bodhi to her catacombs beneath Athkatla, where killing her finally frees Imoen's soul and earns you the Rhynn Lanthorn.

From there, you must enter Suldanessellar to confront Irenicus, a battle which begins beneath the city's palace, amid the branches of the sacred Tree of Life and ends in the Nine Hells, a demonic underworld where you must reclaim your soul if you wish to return to the land of the living.

In *Baldur's Gate II*, these are the islands provided by the game's writers, and in these locations the player will find the stakes higher than anywhere else, the story at its most personal. Your party members have more dialogue during these quests, and can be guaranteed to react to your decisions and to the unfolding of the plot more often than they do elsewhere. In between these islands lie an ocean of choices which every player will have to navigate in his or her own way, and by the time you get to the end of the game, your own version of the above plot is likely to be sagging with details, loose in places where a novelist or filmmaker would have preferred it to remain taut.

The story will be messy but it will also be *yours,* the experience belonging to you in a way that the stories in novels or films usually can't.

By the end of Chapter Two, your experience of the game's story will not resemble mine. There are too many variables, too many possibilities for what comes next. Not only do you have the opportunity to tackle events in almost any order, but so many are optional that you and I will probably not see the same content. Even if we followed the exact same series of events, so much of the game relies on random chance—the digital roll of invisible dice. Your world will not be my world, and the variance between our experiences might be the game's greatest accomplishment. It's also the greatest difficulty the game's writers faced as storytellers. How do you make an emotionally engaging and tension-rich story when characters might wander off in any direction at any moment?

Gameplay limitations such as these can also complicate characterization in unexpected ways. For instance, because your party can never contain more than six characters, rescuing Imoen in Spellhold means you either have to arrive with only five party members (a strategic disadvantage) or you have to leave someone behind if you want to add Imoen to your party. In my playthrough, I only need one mage/thief character, and so I choose to abandon Nalia, even though she's journeyed beside me for most of the game. Unfortunately, because it's not possible for Nalia to find her own way out of the asylum without messing with the plot, my only choice is to tell her to wait where she is until we come back for her, a promise we're doomed to break, because once we leave Spellhold there's no way to return.

I'd known this moment was coming, so I've already stripped Nalia of all of her equipment and weapons—all of which Imoen will also be able to use, since they share the same class. Thankfully, no enemies will attack Nalia while I'm gone, since nothing happens when I'm not in the room. In a way, she'll be safer here than ever before. As we run back and forth through Spellhold, solving puzzles and securing our escape, we frequently return to the room where we left Nalia, still stuck in her idle animation, weaponless and alone, waiting for us to once again invite her to join our party. I hurry my band of adventurers past her as quickly as possible, trying to pay her no mind.

Sorry, friend.

•

In June of 2010—a couple of months after Matthew and I began drafting *The Last Garrison*—I also started traveling weekly from Michigan to New York City for a class with the writer and editor Gordon Lish, held at the Center for Fiction in Manhattan. Most famous for his aggressive cuts to Raymond Carver's early short stories, Lish conducts notoriously intense classes, each one a performance of sorts, usually structured as a lecture delivered with great intensity on a wide range of literary topics, then a critique session where students read their own work aloud to the group. Lish frequently cuts students off as soon as he feels they've made a mistake, which in practice means each person tends to read very little, because there are so many mistakes to be made and because his standards are very high.

Every Monday morning that summer, I flew out of Detroit at six in the morning, arriving in the city by nine or so, with a return flight scheduled for the same time the next day. I spent those Mondays writing in a cubicle at the Center for Fiction during the morning and afternoon, then attending class upstairs from five to midnight, where I often took thousands of words worth of handwritten notes, referencing a world of writers and philosophers and editors I wanted desperately to understand, and where every week in class I presented new work that Lish invariably shot down, disparaged, or otherwise dismissed.

It felt like a fateful bit of luck that the financial cost of Lish's class was exactly the same as my advance from Wizards of the Coast. And so my advance made it possible for me to attend without too much financial burden, most likely making me the only person ever to pay for one of Lish's classes with money earned writing about elves.

I hadn't realized it before we signed our contracts, but Wizards of the Coast had been purchased by Hasbro, the same toy company whose G.I. Joe and Star Wars figures had defined my childhood, and so when my advance check arrived it had seemed to come directly from my past. To push myself through the process, I came to think of writing the D&D book as one last thing I had to do to complete those years, not to escape the childhood I was always trying to leave behind but to acknowledge its power one more time. And in doing so, my past would help me buy the future I desired. In the years before, I'd slowly realized that many of the contemporary writers I most admired had passed through Lish's classes sometime in the 90s, including writers like Christine Schutt, Michael Kimball, Ben Marcus, Dawn Raffel, Brian Evenson, and Sam Lipsyte. And so when the chance came to take his class, I thought of it as an opportunity to see what those writers had gained there, to see if I might take away something similar.

It was not an easy summer, between the travel and the demands of the class, but it was an important one for me. I learned more in those classes than I had in any other chunk of my writer's education. When I was very young, I learned the word *charisma* by reading my dad's D&D rulebooks, those blue and red introductions to that world, but back then I didn't really understand what the word meant. Later I learned what charisma was by studying with Gordon Lish. When he was at his best, it was intoxicating to be in the same room with him, witnessing a complex performance that all the legends and rumors about him still fail to exactly capture.

What I remember most is how emotionally dangerous that class felt to be in, because education so rarely feels dangerous in any way. Never before had I been in a room with a man with this forceful of a personality, and I knew that even while trying to be guarded I was giving up more of myself than I wanted, becoming too eager for his approval, for the praise he doled out so sparingly. The increasing want to please my teacher became a risk I didn't want to take. Despite my admiration, I kept my distance, didn't talk to him much before or after class, trying always to take what I could get without giving up anything else. But I still learned so much, even from my removed demeanor. Lish talked often about writing out of the "wound," whatever original injury we had that if revealed might fuel our writing. In his class, the piece of my writing he praised the most was part of a very short story I wrote about the first lie I could remember telling, when I was four or five. That was one wound, one original crime.

Another wound I continue to carry is the deep shame I sometimes feel about who I was and what I was interested in when I was a child, as a teenager, as an adult: how the fantasy novels and the role-playing and the video games don't match cleanly to the image I've tried to cultivate as a "serious" man, as a writer of fiction, a professor, and an editor.

I have never been truly able to stomach any version of myself except the most present. I pretend that all the past selves are not still with me, that I have shed those skins as I've molted, instead of acknowledging that it's what I've retained from each of my past selves that has made me *me*, that who I am now will make me the person I hope I'm still capable of becoming.

Despite my creeping misgivings during the writing of *The Last Garrison*—despite similar misgivings about writing this book you are reading—I now suspect that one way to end the injury I did to myself by hiding what I loved is to reveal the shame I felt publicly, to put that admission into writing and to make it public.

This book you're holding is one way for me to say, *This is who I was*. It is also, in almost every important way, *still who I am*.

•

Among the many innovations *Baldur's Gate II* brought to the RPG genre was its optional romantic storylines, a feature that BioWare would refine and build upon in most of the games that followed. The romances in *BG2* are more rudimentary than in the company's later games, but even in this first iteration four paramours were made available for the player, three intended for male characters and one for female characters, each with their own storyline. If your Gorion's Ward is male, then he might fall in love with Aerie, the once-winged elf mage/cleric you rescue from the beleaguered circus in Waukeen's Promenade who lost her wings while locked in a cage at the circus; Jaheira, the half-elf druid warrior working for the fabled Harpers, your longtime mentor, and the widow of your dead friend, Khalid; and Viconia, the only evil character among the love interests, a drow cleric you save from being burned at the stake by a racist mob in the Temple District. For female incarnations of Gorion's Ward, there is only Anomen, a human fighter/cleric who wishes to become a knight.

Curiously, all four of the available love interests are spellcasters, and three of the four have at least some elven heritage. All four potential paramours are unconcerned with your profession, and you do not have to be strong or intelligent, nor do you need to be or particularly charismatic. For the most part, only Gorion's Ward's gender and race affect which romances are available, as the four potential paramours will only fall in love with other elves, half-elves, and humans, leaving dwarves, gnomes, halflings, and half-orcs entirely unnoticed.

There are also no same-sex romances in *Baldur's Gate II*, an oversight BioWare games later remedied with party members open to dating both genders. The recently released *Dragon Age: Inquisition* is the first BioWare game to include what *DA:I* writer David Gaider—also one of the writers for *BG2*—called a "fully gay" party member. It's taken a regrettably long time to reach a point where this is possible, but it's also partially a sign of changing attitudes toward depictions of sexuality and gender not just in games but in all media. As Gaider said, "When the romances in *Baldur's Gate II* were made, I didn't even think to suggest we should include same-sex romances… because why would you? It just wasn't done."

As Gorion's Ward, it doesn't matter to the game who else you might be interested in, inside the party or out, or what the quality of your character might be. Regardless of the choices you make elsewhere, you can always fall in love, as long as you're straight, as long as you're human, or an elf or an half-elf, and as long as you want to fall in love with Aerie, Jaheira, Viconia, or Anomen.

But you cannot initiate the romance. The best you can do is invite them to follow you around Amn, hoping sooner or later they'll notice you.

And they do, every single time.

You can fall in love, as long as you're willing to wander screen to screen, waiting for one of the only four lovers in Faerûn to speak. The four lovers, who have eyes only for you. If you're a man, there is no risk of losing Jaheira or Viconia or Aerie to Anomen, even after you've chosen which of the women you'd like to date— and even though the elven female version of Gorion's Ward, who looks just like the three female lovers, is irresistible to him. If you're a woman, only Anomen will ever express interest in you, despite the many other men you travel alongside.

But what if you're a gnome who makes all the exact same choices as your elven counterpart?

Then you are doomed to be disappointed. Even though you may have many fine qualities, you will never find love, at least not in this world.

The romances are a kind of puzzle, like most everything in *Baldur's Gate II*, and while BioWare's later romances seem almost impossible to fail unless you deliberately set out to sabotage them, *BG2*'s are more delicate affairs, easily broken. Assuming you're a suitable match, each love interest will approach you at some point in your journey, striking up dialogues that will increase in romantic fervor over time if you make the right choices. Aerie, for instance, generally needs to be comforted and assured of your goodness (and also reassured that her missing wings do not make her ugly), while Jaheira wants her grief for Khalid to be respected and for you to acknowledge the gravity of your quest. Viconia is the trickiest conversationalist, requiring a more complex mix of affection and aggression, while Anomen mostly needs his ego stroked.

An example of how these flirtations work:

In an early conversation with Gorion's Ward, Aerie says, "My wings have been clipped... Oh, I wish you could understand how it feels to be bound and chained to the ground, like a miserable prisoner of earth."

To which you might reply: "What was it like to fly, Aerie?"

Or: "We're all prisoners of the earth down here."

Or: "If you're going to whine do it somewhere else."

For the purposes of continuing the romance, the best answer is the first one, in which you express interest in Aerie's life. She continues: "I remember I used to be so happy. The clouds are a special place up there... it's like a land of billowing white beauty that you can almost walk on."

Most of your dialogues with Aerie—or with Jaheira or Vicona or Anomen—follow a similar pattern. Show interest long enough and eventually your conversations will lead to expressions of affection, then open romance, then professions of love and sexual invitations. Sex isn't depicted in-game, as in later BioWare titles, but instead promised as an eventual end goal. Make enough effort—and don't make any mistakes—and one day an elven spellcaster will invite you into her tent to spend the night, probably outside some ruin you've spent the past week trapped inside, slaughtering and being slaughtered.

Unfortunately, once you "win" a romance, there's nothing more to do with that character. Your lover will follow you wherever you go, but they would have done this anyway, like any other party member. They can be dismissed from your party or allowed to perish in battle, and no matter what happens no one will comment on it. Any lingering affection you feel will be yours alone, expressed only in the way you interact with the sprites under your care. For their part, your partner will never mention their affection for you again, except in one or two scripted moments at the end of the game.

This playthrough, I'm traveling with both Jaheira and Aerie, which means both of their romance scripts often advance at the same time, so that as soon as I finish a conversation progressing one relationship, the other woman speaks up to take her turn. As our conversations progress, I begin to feel increasingly uneasy, professing Gorion's Ward's growing affection for each woman while the other stands nearby. It's not great timing, but when we enter the graveyard district to confront Bodhi and the rest of her vampire guild, Aerie starts a conversation that forces me to choose between her and Jaheira. I sit and consider my options for a while, letting the dialogue choice linger on the screen while I make my decision. After I choose Jaheira, Aerie is heartbroken but stays in the party. From a gameplay perspective, there is no loss. But I've known this moment was coming for a long time now, and I admit to feeling guilt-ridden now that it's over.

Afterward, Aerie's sprite lingers beside mine, her sling in hand, her gold robe and blue cloak twisting in the digital wind. Part of me wonders if it wouldn't be better for everyone involved if I sent Aerie away.

But definitely not before the fight with Bodhi.

And afterward? Aerie travels with me until the very end. There is no cost to leading her on and then rejecting her, and so I keep her in my party for the rest of the game. But she speaks less now, our heart-to-heart conversations finished forever. If Aerie bears a grudge, she does not mention it. If she ever still thinks of Gorion's Ward fondly, or if she ever regrets what happened between us, she does not mention these thoughts either. And if I feel the same regret, there is no way for the game to let me tell her. A choice has been made and it cannot be undone. All the consequences happen off-screen, inside the player.

This is how games work. The world exists purely for your enjoyment. Everything that happens there is for you or from you. Each of these romances have has been designed for your pleasure and gratification, by a team of writers who innovated storytelling and player investment in the RPG genre in part by creating a game system out of the act of falling in love, a system which asks players to treat prospective partners as puzzles, extended emotional boss battles. Asking players to study their lovers' patterns, to learn their weak spots. But once you win the love of your partner, what then?

A puzzle does not continue to generate interest once you know its solution.

All you can possibly want next is another puzzle.

•

In Milan Kundera's *The Curtain,* his book-length essay on the art of the novel, he writes of wanting novels to emulate "the beauty of a sudden density of life," a departure from the banal normality of life that results from a "personal adventure resulting from some unexpected confluence of opportunities, surprises, lightning seductions."

Even taking into account the ways in which the story can become distended, it's this "sudden density of life" that video games provide so well, and *Baldur's Gate* and its successors at BioWare at first seem to succeed wildly at creating such an experience. When the game truly begins in Waukeen's Promenade, there are adventures *everywhere*. Every few steps through the fog of war there is another enemy, another clickable chest, another quest-giver, here to uphold the illusion of the limitless world. At least at first, it is impossible to walk across any screen of the map without running into someone to save, someone to betray, or someone to fight. Every city or village you enter is filled with people who need help from you, who want to send you across the game world on another quest. Each quest you accept is another commitment to living through another story, to being inside another series of dialogues and battles strewn across another hand-painted screen.

And yet sooner or later the game becomes boring too, a side effect of its inability to accommodate summary through a more modern version of fast travel, which would cut down dramatically on the amount of time you spend watching your party cross a screen now emptied of enemies. If you play the game as a good-aligned character, you are often cast in the role of a protector, a savior. But the more quests you complete, the emptier the game world becomes. Everything you do leaves Faerûn a less interesting place, robbed of danger and conflict.

This is a world created only for you.

You save the world but after it is saved it is always less than it was before.

As you progress through the game, event density goes down. You scurry about, completing sidequest after sidequest, but soon everywhere you go you find only the late-game bleakness of now-empty maps, screens utterly emptied of enemies. Walking across screens utterly emptied of enemies. With nothing new to kill, with no unopened chests, with no one else to talk to, the world becomes a sort of gorgeous void. The same eagle cries and soars overhead again, repeating the same circuitous flight path. The rain always falls at the same angle. There are fireflies in the night, lanterns flickering beneath the earth. A river meanders back and forth. Your party walks and walks. If you are a completionist, you pass the cursor over the screen again and again, pixel-hunting for unopened containers. The clock in the lower-left corner swings its pendulum. Time passes. An hour goes by, then another, then a dozen, then a dozen dozen. No one ages except you, the player.

Even in a game I return to often, the further into the game I progress, the less I remember. Over the years, I started the game more often than I finished it— and I always know that one day the idea of taking on another quest will make me feel a little sick, thanks to the endless to-do list of the adventuring class, the way grinding eventually turns fun into work. Even if each individual quest is fun, there will come a time when you will not want more quests. In the last chapters of *Baldur's Gate II*, the stakes have never been higher, but by then there is also less and less to do and see, until all that awaits you are the final confrontations.

With the once-flush game world exhausted of its potential, I at last return to the main quest, eager for the excitement of the early game to return. Entering the maps that comprise the game's final chapter should be a moment of triumph, but it can also be a moment of exhaustion—when you at last admit there's nothing much left to do. The move toward the ending is not so much an urgency of story as much as it is a craving for a return to a world alive with possibility, where every step brings you into some new conflict, some possible excitement, a change from the increasingly deadened Forgotten Realms.

•

I ran into Gordon Lish outside of class just once that summer, in a restaurant on the corner of the street where the Center for Fiction was located. I knew he sometimes met other students there before our class began, working with them one-on-one on the pages they would later share when we were all together, so I checked to make sure he wasn't there before ordering my food. Somehow I missed him and several of my classmates, and by the time I saw them I'd already ordered and it was too late to try to get my dinner elsewhere.

When Lish saw me typing on my MacBook in the corner of the room, he invited me to join him and the others, to show him what I was writing. I did not accept. I couldn't show him the document I had loaded on my laptop, an early chapter of *The Last Garrison*. Two months into the class, Lish was still very hard on the work I brought to class, new work I'd spent hours honing, trying to put into practice what he'd taught me.

As tough as he was on those stories, I can only imagine what he would have said if I'd shown him *The Last Garrison.*

At the very least, he would have belittled me, and more than likely he would have been cruel about it again in class later that night.

When I think about Lish, I often think too about "What We Talk About When We Talk About Love," one of my favorite Raymond Carver stories he edited and perhaps the most famous, which was once nearly twice as long and titled "Beginners." During the editing process, Lish cut it drastically: He changed character names, rewrote parts, and even removed eight consecutive paragraphs at the end. It's a heavier edit than most editors would feel comfortable suggesting, and Carver later objected to the edits throughout the book of the same name, saying that the cuts to his stories were akin to trying to shove a body into a too-small coffin, complete with the "surgical amputation and transplant that might make them someway fit into the carton so the lid will close." But in the end Carver accepted Lish's edits, and the book was published to enormous critical success, with the critic Michael Wood writing in *The New York Times* that, "in Mr. Carver's silences, a good deal of the unsayable gets said." Only at least some of those "silences" weren't Carver's, but Lish's, under whose guidance this story and others became something less expositional and more ambiguous—and often more interesting, at least to my tastes.

Now there is a part of me that wonders what a page of Lish-edited Dungeons & Dragons novel might have looked like, had I been willing to show him and had he deigned to apply his pen to such "low" art: How might the exposition-heavy, sometimes ponderous world of D&D have changed under his minimalist approach?

Regardless, the summer I spent in Lish's class set the bar for my own writing much higher than anything I was churning out in *The Last Garrison*. I was occasionally having fun writing my fantasy novel, but I knew it wasn't the kind of work I dreamed of doing— I'd reserved my real efforts for the novel I was drafting alongside it, which would become my first published novel under my own name. That was the book I was proud of, the one I wanted to be known for.

After all, one of Lish's favorite tactics was to constantly remind us that one day we would die, and that when we died our writing was one of the only things about us that might live on. What would we leave behind? What would our words say about us, for us?

V

"No! Say it is not so! We will no longer fight evil together? Boo will miss you, Gorion's Ward. Forever shall we hang our heads in sadness in remembrance of our great butt-kicking friend."

—Minsc

ONE HUNDRED THIRTY-FIVE GAME DAYS after Gorion's Ward woke up in Jon Irenicus's dungeon, my party charges the ornate gold and silver gates of the elven palace in Suldanessellar, ready to pursue Irenicus to our final confrontation among the branches of the Tree of Life. From here, there is no turning back, no escape, no way out but through. My version of Gorion's Ward is a 14th level fighter/mage, and my other characters have achieved even higher levels of ability, with Anomen at the 23rd level and Imoen at the 19th. My characters have hit the experience cap of *Baldur's Gate II*—2,950,000 XP—and kept going, thanks to the installed *Throne of Bhaal* expansion, giving us access to the most powerful spells in the game, including some that wouldn't have appeared in the vanilla version of *BG2*.

We could not be more prepared for the fights to come, and yet I'm saving my game now every few feet of movement, loathe to have to redo anything.

On the way to the palace gates, my friends frequently fall in battle—Minsc, my damage-soaking tank, being the most common casualty—only to be raised and sent back into the fight. Imoen casts spells like Simulacrum, calling into being a near-identical clone of herself complete with the ability to cast most of her spells, while Jaheira fills the battlefield with summoned elementals who soak up most enemy attacks and deal huge amounts of damage. The battlefield is now a frenzy of death-dealing clouds and chained lightning bolts and meteor swarms called down from the heavens, each battle more chaotic than the one before.

There's a wish fulfillment aspect of D&D where, over the course of a campaign, the powerless become the powerful. And here that wish is fulfilled: Every weapon used against us has been looted and put to use. Every suit of armor that once blocked our blows now protects our flesh. Every spell cast against us, every summoned creature or magical defense, all of those tools are now ours to use as we will. This deadly acquisition of ability is the cornerstone of D&D: Kills equal experience, experience equals progression, progression equals power.

Earlier in *BG2*, Minsc was the most efficient killer, but he's long since been overtaken. The nominal hero, my Gorion's Ward has proven the most effective butcher this world has made, and with every click of the mouse I send him after more death, which the story tries valiantly to justify. At every previous juncture, choosing the good route over the evil one barely slowed the killing, and so despite my attempts at goodness there can be no doubt that Bhaal, God of Murder and my character's true father, must surely be pleased with the work I've done to fulfill the destiny latent in my blood.

Inside the elven palace, the fabled Tree of Life awaits, "a palpable feeling of magic" emanating from its branches. As you approach the stairs leading down to its branches, the narrator explains that you feel:

> a familiar touch which you instinctively recognize as your own soul. Irenicus is near… You pause, knowing that you may not survive the battle to come. You have little choice, however—without your soul, your fate is a grim and certain one. You turn and regard those who remain in your party. You feel a need, perhaps, to ascertain their loyalty, their friendship, or to offer a chance to reconsider.

One by one you address your party members: Imoen, "your sister and steadfast friend"; Minsc, "the scarred and loyal ranger, always ready to leap into battle with Boo ever at his side"; Aerie, "at times innocent, at times determined," who has "come so far since you took her from the circus in Athkatla"; Anomen, "cleric of the Helm and hearty warrior"; and Jaheira, with whom

Gorion's Ward has "grown close and been through much."

This is the culmination of the romance plot weaved throughout my playthrough of *Baldur's Gate II*, and now Gorion's Ward can't find the words he or she wants to speak. But perhaps it's not necessary to say anything else, as each of your party members reaffirms their reasons for journeying beside you, lending you their unconditional support in your darkest hour. It's one of the most emotional moments of the game, sorely needed after hours of pitched battle. Not everything that could be said is said, but what is said must be enough.

•

When Matthew Simmons and I at last completed a draft of *The Last Garrison*, our editor gave us plenty of notes on specific passages but only one overarching guideline: We had to make it less complicated.

In practice, this mostly meant making sentences simpler—fewer conjunctions, less complex syntax—as well as writing additional exposition and explanation, so no one would misunderstand the plot or the characterization. This was some of the most difficult work, in part because my literary fiction tends to try to cut back on exposition and explanation as much as possible, often using the reader's existing knowledge and imagination to fill in the gaps, as well as letting the logic of the story happen in the reader rather than on the page. By contrast, many fantasy novels—especially the kind of licensed novels set in established worlds like D&D—thrive on exposition: Like the Baldur's Gate games, most stories in the fantasy genre are fairly simple quest narratives, where a hero travels from point to point, completing quests on his or her way to a final confrontation with a particularly imposing foe. Instead of the story or the writing style, it's most often the setting of each individual book that sets it apart from another—the writer's particular combination of fantasy races, invented locations, styles of swordplay, systems of magic and so on—and only the most talented writers can do a lot of worldbuilding without getting bogged down in exposition.

In *The Last Garrison*, we were not always those writers.

If it hadn't been for Matthew Simmons's continual enthusiasm and his pep talks keeping me going, I'm not sure I would have been able to finish. In so many ways, the heart of *The Last Garrison* is more his than mine, and I credit him with the book's best qualities. As for my own contributions, the part of *The Last Garrison* I'm most proud of writing is on pages 172-175. To amuse myself while drafting, I'd started writing imitations of different writers, and in this chapter there's a Samuel Beckett-inspired passage where the party must make their way up a mountain path while undoing or exposing a series of illusions and traps. It was the most fun I had writing the whole book. If I could have found a way to imbue all of my writing in *The Last Garrison* with so much energy, it might have become something much better.

My other favorite part of the book is the dedication, a nod to the dual identity of Matthew Beard: "For my girlfriend Abby and my wife Jessica." It's perhaps the cleverest choice Matthew Beard ever made.

•

In the Underland beneath Suldanessellar, my party rushes to the center of the Tree of Life, where Irenicus waits and where Suldanessellar's Queen Ellesime is held prisoner. As always, Irenicus is indignant at our arrival: "You live *yet*?! You have less than a fraction of your soul, and yet somehow you *continue* to oppose me? The power… the power of the Tree is gone from me. You have been successful in your little scheme, insect, but now this ends! I will take great pleasure in eradicating such a nuisance as you. And then I shall… reestablish my link, join with the Tree once again… I shall find a way, I shall *have* the power—"

"No," Ellesime interrupts, once we've freed her from her cage. "You shall not. Twice now you have attempted this sacrilege and nearly destroyed us all. You will not do this again, Joneleth."

Not even the sound of his elven name moves Irenicus to reconsider the path before him. His pointed ears have long been clipped, his shameful mutilation too long hidden under his spiked skullcap. "There is nothing else beyond my revenge," he cries.

Our assault begins with a flurry of magical attacks, with my spellcasters firing Haste spells and summoning elementals and demons, plus debuffing spells like Breach and Pierce Magic to take down the layers of shield magics making Irenicus nearly invulnerable. For his own part, Irenicus lets loose a series of triggered magics—Fire Shield and Globe of Invulnerability and Mislead—before casting Time Stop and going on the attack with Spellstrike, Power Word Kill, Ice Storm, and other damage-dealing or instadeath spells. The battle is as chaotic as it is quick, and not everyone survives—Imoen falls in battle, struck down by Irenicus as a final insult after his torturing her in his dungeon and in Spellhold. But eventually, when Irenicus is close to death, I pull back the other characters to let Gorion's Ward strike the final blow, an unnecessary but personally important gesture.

"*You* k-killed me," he says. "T-this is not... this... is not..."

As Irenicus's body crumples, the narrator speaks: "A strange quiet envelopes the scene. You begin to wonder if you have finally won, if it is all truly over. You feel a small tug inside yourself, a pull that seems to come from the apparition that rose from Irenicus. It is gentle at first, but quickly becomes urgent. Within seconds, you cannot breathe, drawn inexorably to where Irenicus fell. You are still connected to your stolen soul, but it is no longer among the living. Released in death, your stolen soul does not return to you. It is falling away from the mortal world, and you are being dragged along with it."

Fire engulfs you. Soon you've left the mortal realm for the Nine Hells, one underworld of the Forgotten Realms. Somewhere in these Nine Hells, Irenicus still owns some portion of your soul, and you'll have to traverse this underworld if you hope to recover it and return to the land of the living.

You see before you a nightmarish door—its joints seemingly a collection of interlocked and terrible teeth—guarded by five giant eyeballs. Everywhere you look, another horror fills the screen, every room the color of blood, decorated by statues of horned creatures cut into the rocks, their mouths grimacing, their eyes put out. The Nine Hells are the domain of Bhaal, Gorion's Ward's true father, and it's here that you'll once again either accept or reject that heritage.

There are five pathways leading away from the main chamber of the Nine Hells, and the first leads to a winged demon named Pride, who waits in a chamber decorated with bloodshot eyeballs and fanged mouths, dead branches shaped like clutching clawed hands, and other terrible sights. Elsewhere statues of horned creatures are cut into the rocks, their mouths grimacing, their eyes put out.

The demon explains that to seek my soul is to undergo a series of trials, with each trial having both a good and an evil solution. By these trials we will be judged, and when we are finished we will have earned the five Tears of Bhaal needed to open the great door of the Nine Hells, beyond which our soul—and Irenicus—awaits. For his part, Pride tries to convince us to kill the guardian of its Tear, but we refuse until the frustrated demon says we have no pride ourselves, despite our great need: "Humility serves well those who wield it well." Pride disappears, revealing a friendly dragon, one who will give us the Tear without a fight.

We climb back up the stairs and begin the other trials: Fear, Selfishness, Greed. Each is guarded by a demon who forces us to make the difficult choice of virtue or vice—and as tempting as the evil solutions are, we can collect the Tears without giving up our goodness. But completing the trials is the only way to earn Gorion's

Ward's path out of this hell, a place at least partially of his or her own making.

Only the Trial of Wrath lacks a demon. Instead we meet the wraith of our Bhaal-brother Sarevok, last killed a hundred real-life hours ago at the end of *Baldur's Gate*. "How fitting," he says, "that our reunion should be in this place of retribution." Like many other enemies in *BG2*, Sarevok taunts you, trying to "stoke that infernal wrath," an anger "boiling like a pit of sulfur in the crevices of your heart," hoping to force you to become again the Slayer, the avatar of Bhaal. Only by refusing—by choosing pity instead of wrath—can you stay on the path of good.

Whatever choice you make, Sarevok must be defeated one more time. You kill and kill your enemies but they do not stay dead and so the killing never ends.

•

I still have two crates of fantasy novels and D&D rulebooks in my office closet, books I haven't read in years even though I've moved them from house to house and now across the country from Michigan to Arizona. Why aren't these fantasy novels on display somewhere in my house, where there are a thousand-plus other books stacked across a dozen bookshelves? Because bookshelves do more than just hold up our books. They speak to how we see ourselves, and more obviously how we want others to see us. This is a part of my makeup I don't always show.

Part of why I wanted to write this book was to once again try to shake off this shame I should not have to feel. When I was growing up, almost everything I loved was deeply uncool and embarrassing, and so I learned, year by year, to hide more of that part of me away. To pretend I was not into fantasy and science fiction and Dungeons & Dragons. To never talk about computer games in class or on the school bus. I was writing a little then but it wouldn't last because I couldn't show it to anyone other than my brother. I believed then that the person I wanted most to become wasn't someone other people would accept—at least not without teasing comments—and so I pretended to be someone else whenever I stepped outside of the house.

One of the major turning points in my own writing was when I started letting in some of these fantasy and science fiction influences again, which for most of my twenties I kept out of my fiction. As soon as I did so, my writing opened up, became more mine, stronger than anything else I'd written. In *How They Were Found,* my first book of stories, there are stories about post-apocalyptic military outposts, about mechanical messiahs, about tiny doppelgangers who appear in the wake of a breakup, about girlfriends who disappear into other dimensions rather than succumb to terminal illness. When I let back in the kind of fantastic and fabulist stories I'd grown up on, it almost immediately resulted in more lively fiction than I'd been making in the years before. I was using all of my imagination instead of just the portion I thought would be acceptable to others.

When I teach younger writers, one of the things I try to stress is how to not give up what's weird or quirky or strange about yourself, about the way your mind works. The writing workshop can sometimes have a leveling effect, with a student's story being subjected to other people's ideas of what is good or smart or acceptable, and I try to combat this by seeking out the quirk in each piece of writing so that in revision I might ask students to try turning up the volume on that part of the story. Every story we see in class, regardless of its level of accomplishment, has at least one move that maybe no one else would make, and part of my job seems to be to point out what's different about each student's work, then task them with exploring the weirdness in their imagination instead of turning away or hiding it. This is what's worked in my own writing, but it took me so long to understand it: My writing can't be brought to life by a denial of how I'm different than others, but instead requires the exploration of that difference.

It seems so easy. All you have to do is figure out how to become the best version of yourself, the person you truly want to be, in a world that encourages conformity, that prizes productivity over personality. But while I can apply this principle to my art, I am less talented at practicing it in the rest of my life, where I still care way too much about what other people think of me.

•

The trials completed, Gorion's Ward sets the five Tears of Bhaal in the five giant eyeballs surrounding the mawed door in the central chamber of the Nine Hells. As the last tear is placed, the door opens and Irenicus appears in blast of fire and lightning.

"So, we are to battle one last time," Irenicus says. "No more hiding for either of us. I will enjoy destroying you… To die in this place is to cease to exist! As horrific as this place is, it merely mirrors the soul we now share. Shrink from it if you will, but I have grown to appreciate what it can offer! Now defend yourself! One of us is not truly dead and may be restored if the other is left here to rot! I will be free with what I have taken!'"

"I am ready to face you," says Gorion's Ward, at my command. "I have seen the depths of my soul and I am not afraid."

As always, my friends are there beside me, ready to follow me to the very end, Jaheira, Imoen, Anomen, Aerie, and of course Minsc: "I grow tired of shouting battle cries when fighting this mage. Boo will finish his eyeballs once and for all so he does not rise again! Evil, meet my sword! SWORD, MEET EVIL!"

I take the mouse in my hand, move the cursor over Irenicus, watch it become a sword signifying my character's intent, then click once, my action in reality unpausing this virtual world.

In the Nine Hells, the last battle begins, a multiverse of choices narrowing toward a single shared conclusion: We will triumph and Irenicus will fall.

Irenicus summons a legion of demons and other extraplanar creatures to fight for him, then transforms into the Slayer, the fearsome avatar of Bhaal you have refused to become. The Slayer is a dreadful enemy, with an incredible immunity to magic, plus deadly physical attacks and the ability to regenerate health. He also retains some of Irenicus's spellcasting abilities, although thankfully not the Time Stop spells that were so deadly before.

Aerie falls, struck down by one of the demons, but Anomen resurrects her mid-fight to allow her to immediately rejoin the attack on the Slayer. Jaheira calls a prince of the elemental planes to join our side, and Imoen fills the battlefield with devas and pit fiends, forcing angels and demons alike into her service. My version of Gorion's Ward has a foot in both the martial and the magical arts, and Minsc has earned *Throne of Bhaal*'s Whirlwind Attack ability, allowing him to attack ten times in a single combat round.

We attack and retreat and attack again and hit point by hit point we drive back the Slayer and its demons. As soon as it's defeated, the Slayer disappears, once again revealing the figure of Jon Irenicus, the broken man, the fallen elf. Here at the end of his life, Irenicus's failure is made all the more pathetic by our incredible display of the kind of power he had hoped to take himself.

Our deathly pursuit of Irenicus has made us more powerful than anyone, and has taken us into the pantheon of gods he aspired to ascend to. And after Irenicus's death a path to true godhood will open to us in *Throne of Bhaal*. Along with the actions of our half-brother Sarevok, vanquished once in *Baldur's Gate* and revanquished in the Nine Hells, Irenicus's challenge has taken Gorion's Ward from his humble origins and forced him into becoming exactly what Irenicus wished for himself instead.

Without these adversaries, Gorion's Ward might still be living in Candlekeep, reading books about the adventures of others instead of forging his own tales.

•

There's no reason for me to hide anymore.

Much of our popular culture is based in science fiction, comic books, and fantasy, with many of the biggest movies every year being set in future dystopias or fantastical worlds, and video games are widely enjoyed by a huge portion of the population. This past summer, *The New York Times* even published an article titled "A Game as Literary Tutorial," about how a generation of writers has been influenced by D&D, including Junot Díaz, China Miéville, Cory Doctorow, Sherman Alexie, and many others.

What, exactly, is it that I'm hiding?

That I am still, in my heart of hearts, that younger person. That I believe deeply that I am the person my teenage bullies long ago accused me of being: a geek, a nerd, a freak, a weirdo.

Even when I was a kid, I believed that the other kids who teased me weren't saying anything untrue. They were, in many ways, just correctly pointing out that I wasn't one of them. I knew I wasn't but I didn't know what to do about it. If I could go back, I would tell myself to celebrate that difference, to be glad I wasn't like most of the people I grew up beside, who I was stuck with not by choice but by a chance of geography and social class.

What does it mean to still be ashamed of interests that so many other people openly celebrate? What does it mean to still be ashamed of the part of myself that has, in so many ways, bought me my entire career? If I had not been a fantasy reader, a video game player, a D&D dungeon master, I would probably not be a writer or an editor or a professor.

I know this.

I do not always admit it but I am admitting it now.

I wonder what it's cost me to move away from them so often, to refuse so strongly what once mattered so much.

If I am still hiding my fantasy novels, I have at least given up hiding my video games, which anyone visiting my living room can see. In an attempt to separate my workspace from my playspace, I started playing console games exclusively a few years ago. When my colleagues from the university come over to our house, they almost always comment on the number of consoles under the TV, about the rows of games lining the shelves under my turntable in the corner of the room. Video games have never been more popular in the culture at large, but inside my subculture of university professors it sometimes seems they're just as unknown to my peers as PC games were to my sixth grade classmates, playing in the corner of the room while others struggled with their social studies. My fellow professors or other writers come to our house for dinner or to watch a movie, and they never fail to comment: "You have so many video games." I do not tell them how many more there are elsewhere, or how one of the greatest advances in recent gaming technology is how we're now able to buy digital editions of games on Xbox Live, PlayStation Network, and Steam, which allows me to buy new games and keep them out of sight, where no one might suspect just how many games I have played, am playing, will always be playing.

·

On the 140th day of our quest, the soul of Gorion's Ward awakens in Suldanessellar to find Queen Ellesime holding vigil over his own empty body. We have been gone for several days, according to the elves, and no amount of their magic could reverse our state. And yet here we are again, back among the living. Surrounded by the elves of Suldanessellar, we soon stand in the central chamber of the temple, where Ellesime offers a benediction on our behalf, and also a final eulogy for the elf Joneleth, her former lover, and for the evil man he became, Jon Irenicus: "I can only say that he died long ago. He lives in my memory still."

Over the course of this adventure, we have slain hundreds of enemies, collected so many magic swords and axes and halberds and spears. We lugged so many suits of armor to the ends of Faerûn and back without ever wearing them. We memorized so many spells we never cast, all those pages in our spellbooks just the useless artifacts of a wizard's education. Somewhere in our backpacks, we stashed tens of thousands of gold pieces we couldn't find a worthy place to spend.

You are no different. Perhaps your armor is dented, your swords nicked and dulled. Probably your wands lay uncharged and useless, every magical impulse expended in the final battles.

You have been held captive, subjected to torture, had your soul ripped from you. Your friends have suffered the same or worse but you have avenged those you could not save. Your companions have died and been resurrected and then died again. Your intelligence and wisdom have been bartered to demons, your experience stolen by the touch of countless vampires. You have descended into hell and returned to the land of the living and every adversary you have ever met is vanquished into digital dust. You have grown powerful on the blood of the fallen and now you stand on the threshold of godhood, flush with a divine power—one earned, not stolen like Irenicus's.

If a normal person in D&D has just a single hit point, you are now in possession of a life force the equivalent of more than a hundred men, and even that is no adequate measure of your strength.

Surrounded by cheering elves, your avatar stands, a flatness filled only with you and your choices, flanked by the companions who have come so far with you already, who will follow you now to the very end.

Despite all the suffering that has led you to this place, surely you celebrate.

•

When I was younger, I would have given anything to write a real Dungeons & Dragons novel, and now here I am writing about D&D again, making the same choice despite the many other games I might have chosen to write about, despite part of me that wants so desperately to *grow up*—despite evidence I already have, that my love of these hobbies has grown up with me.

In a recent text conversation, I told my brother Nick how often I had tried to give up fantasy novels, video games, and D&D at different stages in my life. He responded immediately that he had never had a moment of what he called "adulthood break," and because of this he's the one who stayed connected to our childhood. For him, growing up didn't mean giving up who he'd been.

At the time of our conversation, Nick was ripping his DVDs of the original *G.I. Joe* cartoon to his hard drive, telling me, "Now I refresh my memories, see if what I remembered matched reality." I didn't tell him that I often experience the opposite emotion. When I watch a show or listen to a song or play a game I liked when I was younger, it's not nostalgia that I feel but shame or embarrassment.

Whenever people talk about the "good old days," I frequently chime in to say that every year my life has gotten closer to the life I wanted to be living. I believe this is true but I'm also protesting too much. By the time I was a teenager, I wanted desperately to be an adult, to be thought of as experienced and intelligent and worldly. As a teenager that meant giving up anything I thought might be considered childish. Later it meant sex, drinking, disobedience—all the small rebellions of the Midwest, the most obvious shortcuts. Then it meant being a good student or a good writer, a good husband and a good teacher, as if I could win my adulthood just by making other people believe I'd done so.

I still get royalty statements every three months from Hasbro. Not royalty checks, unfortunately, just statements letting me know how little the book is selling. It never earned out its advance, and it's clear it never will. But that advance bought me a summer in New York, studying with Gordon Lish, who had taught so many of my favorite writers. And it bought me a year of working with Matthew Simmons, who I had only known a little before we started, but who became a friend as he bravely led me through the adventure of writing a novel together. Most importantly, the book led me to play Dungeons & Dragons again with my brothers, something I hadn't done in at least fifteen years, something I hadn't known how much I had missed.

A final bonus: As far as I know, *The Last Garrison* was the first of my books my dad ever read all the way through. Later, my mom told me he liked it so much he had to pace their living room as he read the last chapters, trying to walk off the finale's suspense. The novel certainly didn't rise to the standard Lish taught me my work should, won't ever be something durable enough to last after I'm gone. But while I am here, it has earned me the education I'd craved, forged a new friendship, brought me closer to my brothers, and made my dad proud.

It's enough.

It's more than I ever hoped Dungeons & Dragons might do.

•

"As for you," Ellesime says, "I imagine you are eager to resume your travels once again."

You have survived but the game has no more agency to offer. Whatever quests you left unfinished will never be completed, at least in this playthrough.

In fact, you will never finish every quest on a single playthrough. Some you never find, some you avoid, some you can't solve. Eventually you get locked into the endgame, maybe without even realizing you've passed the point of no return. There's no going back for anything you've missed. This was your life, and now it's over.

There's no new game plus mode in *Baldur's Gate II*. The end is the end.

The end is the end and yet there are so many places we never traveled together, so many familiar faces from previous playthroughs that this time we never met. In my most recent playthrough, we never journeyed alongside Mazzy Fentan or Jan Jansen or Keldorn Firecam or Cernd or Valygar Corthala or Haer'Dalis. After our first encounters, we never adventured again with Edwin Odesseironor, Viconia DeVir, or Korgan Bloodaxe, or Yoshimo. I never even went back to Spellhold to save my long-time companion Nalia de'Arnise, who is presumably still idling there in the depths, her inventory emptied, her progression stalled out a million or so experience points behind what my party has become.

Most of Gorion's Ward's other stories have to go untold here. I've barely even mentioned what happens to him or her next, in *Throne of Bhaal*, where Gorion's Ward fulfills his or her destiny at the end of the Bhaalspawn Crisis, but even as this book is ending I'm still playing, going on without taking any more notes, without capturing more screenshots or cutscene footage. Once again, my story is mine alone.

But if you're reading this, maybe you already know this story. Maybe you have your own versions of everything I've told you.

Maybe all along you've been saying, *That isn't quite right.*

Maybe you've been saying, *When I was Gorion's Ward...*

And you're right. Things were different then, when you were Gorion's Ward.

But I was Gorion's Ward, too, and this is the latest telling of my story.

In *Baldur's Gate II*, this world we shared, we all had the same adopted father, we all had the same home. Our father was taken from us. Our home lost. We were cast out, barely able to protect ourselves. We needed friends, a party of adventurers to share our path, and we gathered those friends to us. We fell in love, we were betrayed, we were saved a hundred times over. We killed and were killed, we returned from the dead to kill again, to take from the world what we thought we deserved. It wasn't just violence and greed that motivated us, but also a need to do great deeds, to be heroes, to save the world. What new dangers lurked on the next screen or in the next dungeon? Everywhere we went, adventure rose to meet us, accompanied by the sound of a mouse clicking, clicking, clicking.

In true D&D fashion, maybe the best place to share these many adventures would be a tavern, but for now all we have between us is this book. It tells my story but I wish it could tell me yours too. But for that we'd need a better book, a magic book, and those exist only in games, in novels, in the other ways we might come together to imagine new worlds into being.

NOTES

Luke Kristjanson's comments on Imoen's retconning appear in IGN's 2008 retrospective "Baldur's Gate Memories" which can be found at bit.ly/1KpoDvE.

BioWare founders Ray Muzyka and Greg Zeschuk discussed their design philosophy at length in a 2003 feature on GameSpot called "Baldur's Gate II Postgame Wrap-Up," which can be found at http://bit.ly/1J6pmD3.

The Metacritic page for Baldur's Gate II is at bit.ly/1GEuzSn.

Kate Bernheimer's "Fairy Tale is Form, Form is Fairy Tale" originally appeared *The Writer's Notebook: Craft Essays from Tin House* (2009).

Patricia Henley's "write the islands" interview with Andrew Scott was published as "Taking the Soulful Journey: An Interview with Patricia Henley" in *The Writer's Chronicle 35* (May/Summer 2003).

Raymond Carver's short story "What We Talk About When We Talk About Love" first appeared in a 1981 book of the same name. Michael Wood's praise for the story appeared the same year in a *New York Times* review called "Stories Full of Edges and Silences," available at nyti.ms/1FZXLEz. The pre-Gordon Lish draft of "Beginners" was published in the December 24, 2007 issue of *The New Yorker* and can be found at nyr.kr/1GLlkRy. Carver's initial objections to Lish's heavy hand were reported by Simon Armitage in the article "Rough Crossings," published in that very same issue. It can be found at nyr.kr/1d03JIk.

The interview with David Gaider in which he discusses Dorian's sexuality is available on the official Dragon Age site: bit.ly/1HMt1EK. His updated comments on including same-sex romances appear in an opinion article on Polygon titled "A Character Like Me: the lead writer of Dragon Age on inclusive games," which can be found at http://bit.ly/1HMt1EK.

Ethan Gilsdorf's "A Game as Literary Tutorial: Dungeons & Dragons Has Influenced a Generation of Writers" appeared in 2014 in *The New York Times* and is available at nyti.ms/1wlCZoG.

Throughout the writing process, a couple of wikis were especially helpful: The Baldur's Gate Wiki (bit.ly/1QaHP1S) and The Forgotten Realms Wiki (bit.ly/1cjHVH7). And there's a trove of Minsc quotes available at the former minscandboo.com, now accessible at the Internet Archive (http://bit.ly/2ktV5XW).

ACKNOWLEDGEMENTS

Thanks first and foremost to Gabe Durham, without whose effort and encouragement this book would not exist. The final shape of this book owes every debt to you, and I'm so appreciative of your time and talent and vision.

Thanks to Nick Bell, brother, friend, dungeon master, and research partner: Without your undying affection for our childhood, I'd remember so much less of the best years we spent at each other's side. Thanks for preserving one of the greatest parts of my life and for helping me write about it in this book.

Thanks to my dad, for indulging his curiosity 30+ years ago and buying those first D&D books, without which I might never have played; and for giving us free rein with generations of home computers, without which we would have missed so many of our most formative experiences as gamers.

Thanks to Matthew Simmons, the better half of Matthew Beard, for letting me talk about our experience writing *The Last Garrison* here. Thanks also to Luke Bell, Michelle Lester Bell, and Michael Shaffer, for letting me join your party for a few months while writing that book—a finer group of warriors and wizards and uncomfortably sexy druids may never be assembled.

Thanks to everyone on the Boss Fight Books team: to Michael P. Williams, for his editorial assistance and his research skills; to Ken Baumann for his cover design; to Adam Robinson for his interior layout; and to Ryan Plummer, Nick Sweeney, and Joseph M. Owens for their copyediting.

Finally and always, thanks to Jess, for her love, for her support, which have made all my books possible—and for mostly forgetting that one and only time you saw me in my full geek glory, throwing twenty-sided dice and vowing vengeance upon all my imagined enemies, surrounded by a party of adventurers you're now obligated to call your family forever.

SPECIAL THANKS

For making this series possible, Boss Fight Books would like to thank Ken Durham, Jakub Koziol, Cathy Durham, Maxwell Neely-Cohen, Adrian Purser, Kevin John Harty, Gustav Wedholm, Theodore Fox, Anders Ekermo, Jim Fasoline, Mohammed Taher, Joe Murray, Ethan Storeng, Bill Barksdale, Max Symmes, Philip J. Reed, Robert Bowling, Jason Morales, Keith Charles, and Asher Henderson.

ALSO FROM
BOSS FIGHT BOOKS